Microsoft® Project 2010

2010

Level 2

Microsoft® Project 2010: Level 2

Part Number: 084603
Course Edition: 1.0

NOTICES

HELP US IMPROVE OUR COURSEWARE

Your comments are important to us. Please contact us at Element K Press LLC, 1-800-478-7788, 500 Canal View Boulevard, Rochester, NY 14623, Attention: Product Planning, or through our Web site at **http://support.elementkcourseware.com**.

Microsoft® Project 2010: Level 2

Lesson 5: Reusing Project Plan Information

Appendix A: Synchronizing with SharePoint

About This Course

Microsoft® Project 2010: Level 2 is the second course in the Microsoft Project 2010 series. In *Microsoft® Project 2010: Level 1*, you used your project management skills to create a project plan. Because project requirements are constantly changing to meet the needs of business, the plans need to be updated and modified regularly to keep the project moving on track. This course will build upon the Microsoft Project 2010 skills and knowledge you have gained so far, and give you the opportunity to work with a project plan once it reaches the project implementation phase.

A project manager's job includes delivering a quality product on time and within budget, as well as communicating effectively with all the members of the project team. Creating a project plan helps you trace the path that will help you achieve this. However, constant vigilance and keeping the plan updated with the latest information is important to keep track of the progress. Once a plan gets underway, circumstances that affect your team's ability to meet deadlines can arise. This course will help you learn how to monitor and modify your plan regularly to compensate for any such bumps on the road.

Course Description

Target Student

This course is designed for a person who has an understanding of project management concepts, who has the basic skills to create and modify project plans using Microsoft Project 2010, and who needs to use Microsoft Project 2010 to manage and customize those plans through the implementation stage of a project.

Course Prerequisites

Students enrolling in this class should have the ability to create and update project plans using Microsoft Project 2010. You can obtain this level of skills and knowledge by taking the following course:

● Microsoft® Project 2010: Level 1

A general understanding of project management concepts is helpful, but is not required. To obtain this general understanding, you may choose to take the following course:

● Project Management Fundamentals: (Second Edition)

Knowledge of other Microsoft Office 2010 applications would also be helpful, but is not required.

Course Objectives

In this course, you will manage and customize project plans during the implementation stage of a project.

You will:

- Exchange project plan data with other applications.
- Update a project plan.
- Manage project costs.
- Report project data visually.
- Reuse project plan information.

How to Use This Book

As a Learning Guide

This book is divided into lessons and topics, covering a subject or a set of related subjects. In most cases, lessons are arranged in order of increasing proficiency.

The results-oriented topics include relevant and supporting information you need to master the content. Each topic has various types of activities designed to enable you to practice the guidelines and procedures as well as to solidify your understanding of the informational material presented in the course.

At the back of the book, you will find a glossary of the definitions of the terms and concepts used throughout the course. You will also find an index to assist in locating information within the instructional components of the book.

In the Classroom

This book is intended to enhance and support the in-class experience. Procedures and guidelines are presented in a concise fashion along with activities and discussions. Information is provided for reference and reflection in such a way as to facilitate understanding and practice.

Each lesson may also include a Lesson Lab or various types of simulated activities. You will find the files for the simulated activities along with the other course files on the enclosed CD-ROM. If your course manual did not come with a CD-ROM, please go to **http:// elementkcourseware.com** to download the files. If included, these interactive activities enable you to practice your skills in an immersive business environment, or to use hardware and software resources not available in the classroom. The course files that are available on the CD-ROM or by download may also contain sample files, support files, and additional reference materials for use both during and after the course.

As a Teaching Guide

Effective presentation of the information and skills contained in this book requires adequate preparation. As such, as an instructor, you should familiarize yourself with the content of the entire course, including its organization and approaches. You should review each of the student activities and exercises so you can facilitate them in the classroom.

Throughout the book, you may see Instructor Notes that provide suggestions, answers to problems, and supplemental information for you, the instructor. You may also see references to "Additional Instructor Notes" that contain expanded instructional information; these notes appear in a separate section at the back of the book. Microsoft® PowerPoint® slides may be provided in the included course files, which are available on the enclosed CD-ROM or by download from **http://elementkcourseware.com**. The slides are also referred to in the text. If you plan to use the slides, it is recommended to display them during the corresponding content as indicated in the Instructor Notes in the margin.

The course files may also include assessments for the course, which can be administered diagnostically before the class, or as a review after the course is completed. These exam-type questions can be used to gauge the students' understanding and assimilation of course content.

As a Review Tool

Any method of instruction is only as effective as the time and effort you, the student, are willing to invest in it. In addition, some of the information that you learn in class may not be important to you immediately, but it may become important later. For this reason, we encourage you to spend some time reviewing the content of the course after your time in the classroom.

As a Reference

The organization and layout of this book make it an easy-to-use resource for future reference. Taking advantage of the glossary, index, and table of contents, you can use this book as a first source of definitions, background information, and summaries.

Course Icons

Icon	Description
	A **Caution Note** makes students aware of potential negative consequences of an action, setting, or decision that are not easily known.
	Display Slide provides a prompt to the instructor to display a specific slide. Display Slides are included in the Instructor Guide only.
	An **Instructor Note** is a comment to the instructor regarding delivery, classroom strategy, classroom tools, exceptions, and other special considerations. Instructor Notes are included in the Instructor Guide only.
	Notes Page indicates a page that has been left intentionally blank for students to write on.
	A **Student Note** provides additional information, guidance, or hints about a topic or task.
	A **Version Note** indicates information necessary for a specific version of software.

Course Requirements

Hardware

You will need one computer for each student and the instructor. To use Microsoft Project 2010 on each machine, you need the following hardware:

● Intel® 700 MHz or higher processor

● 512 megabytes (MB) of RAM or more

● 6 gigabytes (GB) of available hard-disk space or more

- CD-ROM drive
- 1024 x 768 or higher resolution monitor (Preferred monitor is a wide screen LCD for viewing Project)
- Microsoft® Mouse, Microsoft® IntelliMouse®, or a compatible pointing device
- Projection system to display the instructor's computer screen
- An Internet connection to support automatic updates and product activation

Software

Software required on each machine includes the following:

- Microsoft® Project Professional 2010
- Microsoft® Office 2010
- Microsoft® Windows® XP Professional with Service Pack 3, or Microsoft® Windows® Vista™ Business Edition with Service Pack 1, or Microsoft® Windows® 7

This course was developed using the Microsoft® Windows® XP operating system; however, the manufacturer's documentation states that the Microsoft® Project 2010 application will also run on Windows Vista or Windows 7. If you use Windows Vista or Windows 7, you may notice slight differences when setting up and keying the course.

Class Setup

Install Windows XP

1. Install Windows XP Professional on an empty partition.
   - Leave the Administrator password blank.
   - When prompted, enable automatic updates.
   - For all other installation parameters, use values that are appropriate for your environment (see your local network administrator for details).
2. If you installed Windows XP Professional into a workgroup rather than into a domain, disable the **Welcome** screen. (This step ensures that students will be able to log on as the Administrator user regardless of what other user accounts exist on the computer.)
   a. Click **Start** and choose **Control Panel→User Accounts.**
   b. Click **Change The Way Users Log On And Off.**
   c. Uncheck **Use Welcome Screen.**
   d. Click **Apply Options.**
3. On Windows XP Professional, install Service Pack 3. Use the Service Pack installation defaults.

Install and Configure Microsoft Office 2010 and Microsoft Project Professional 2010

1. Log on to the computer as the Administrator user if you have not already done so.
2. Perform a complete installation of Microsoft Office Professional 2010, with any current service packs.
3. Run the Microsoft Project 2010 installation executable file, click **Install Now,** and follow the prompts in the installation wizard.

4. Once the installation is complete, click **Close.**

5. Launch Project 2010, and if necessary, in the **Welcome to the 2010 Microsoft Office system** dialog box, select **Use Recommended Settings** and then click **OK.**

6. On the Ribbon, choose **File→Options→Trust Center** and then click **Trust Center Settings.** In the left pane, click **Legacy Formats** and select the **Allow loading files with legacy or non default file formats** option and then click **OK** twice to close the project options.

7. Close Project 2010.

Adjust the System Clock

 Changing the system clock date is needed to make the dates in the various data files and activity steps valid.

1. Open the **Date and Time Properties** dialog box.

2. On the **Internet Time** tab, uncheck **Automatically Synchronize with an Internet Time Server.**

3. Set the time and date to no later than July 11, 2011.

4. Open Project 2010.

Install Data Files

1. On the course CD-ROM, run the 084603dd.exe self-extracting file. This will install a folder named 084603Data on your C drive. This folder contains all the data files that you will use to complete this course. If your course did not come with a CD-ROM, please go to **http://www.elementk.com/courseware-file-downloads** to download the data files.

2. Verify that the file extensions are visible. (In Windows Explorer, choose **Tools→Folder Options** and select the **View** tab. If necessary, deselect the **Hide Extensions For Known File Types** option and click **OK.**)

In addition to the specific setup procedures needed for this class to run properly, you should also check the Element K Press product support website at **http://support.elementkcourseware.com** for more information. Any update about this course will be posted there.

List of Additional Files

Printed with each activity is a list of files students open to complete that activity. Many activities also require additional files that students do not open, but are needed to support the file(s) students are working with. These supporting files are included with the student data files on the course CD-ROM or data disk. Do not delete these files.

1 Exchanging Project Plan Data with Other Applications

Lesson Time: 1 hour(s)

Lesson Objectives:

In this lesson, you will exchange project plan data with other applications.

You will:

● Import project information into a new project plan using the Import Wizard.

● Export project plan cost data to an Excel workbook using the Export Wizard.

● Copy a picture of the required project plan information into a Word document.

Introduction

Having created a project plan file in the Project Initiation and Project Planning phases, the file becomes your plan's focal point. By itself, though, a project file is not helpful because few team members will have Project installed to share and view the information that is relevant to them. Fortunately, Project can easily exchange data with various other applications, as well as embed images of project information in other file formats to display and share data with other team members, particularly if they have different requirements for the data you provide. In this lesson, you will exchange project plan data with other applications to help you meet the wide-ranging information requirements of team members.

Each project typically involves the combined efforts of various team members. Therefore, proper communication and organization is a must. To meet these ends, you will frequently work with data in different formats to build the project plan and exchange project information among the team members. The different stakeholders in a project plan will often have different requirements for shared information, and different expectations for how they will stay informed about the project's status. Knowing how to work with different file formats and different ways of sharing information is critical to performing your job as a successful project manager.

TOPIC A
Import Project Information

Microsoft Project can interact with many other applications, and this capability allows you to incorporate data into the project plan from files in different formats. In this topic, you will import project information from other applications.

Assume that you need to include task information in Project using data from an Excel worksheet. Rather than retyping the data and risking the introduction of errors, you can dynamically transfer the Excel worksheet containing the desired data directly to Project. By doing this, you not only avoid data entry mistakes, but also save time. Furthermore, Project allows you to choose the content that is to be inserted into the plan, thereby preventing the potential problem of accidentally deleting some necessary data along with unnecessary data.

Import Formats

Importing is a method of transferring data from a source file in a particular application to a destination file in a different application. Project can import all the data, or only selected data from a file. It can import task, resource, or assignment data into new or existing project plans. The imported data can be manipulated in the project plan without affecting the source file. Project can import various file formats, such as Excel workbooks, Access databases, comma-delimited files, text files, XML files, and Outlook tasks. The **Import Wizard** is triggered for all file formats except Project files and Outlook tasks.

Project 2010 Support for Excel File Formats

Microsoft Project 2010 is the first version of Project that supports importing or exporting files that are saved in the .xlsx file format. Previous versions of Project required that the imported workbook be saved in the Excel 97–2007 format (*.xls), which is no longer necessary.

Import Outlook Tasks

Project can also import task information from Microsoft Office Outlook. To do so, from the **Tools** menu, choose **Import Outlook Tasks,** and in the **Import Outlook Tasks** dialog box, select the tasks you wish to import. However, the user must have an Outlook account to use this option.

Enhanced Copy and Paste

In addition to the ability to import data into and export data from Project, you can use a new copy and paste feature to transfer data between applications or files. Enhanced copy and paste retains formatting, such as outline levels, headings, text formatting, and more.

Maps

Definition:

In Project, a *map* is a set of instructions that traces the type of data that is to be imported or exported, as well as the location where the data is to be imported into a project plan. It enables the user to specify which fields in the source file should correspond to the fields in the destination file. Maps are of two types, import maps and export maps. You can customize the mapping during the import or export process if the default mapping that Project creates based on the field names in the source file are not correct.

Example:

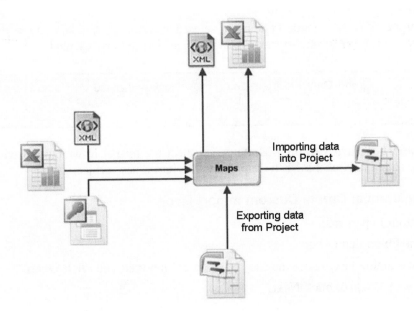

Figure 1-1: Importing and exporting data in Project.

The Import Wizard

In Project, the **Open** dialog box enables you to import files into a project plan. When a file format other than a Project file is opened, the **Import Wizard** is displayed. The **Import Wizard** helps you map data, if you need to adjust the default mapping. This wizard can import selected data or an entire file into a new project plan, or as an addendum to an existing, open project plan. If you customize the mapping, you can save the map for future use.

How to Import Project Information

Procedure Reference: Import a File into a New Project Plan

To import a file into a new project plan:

1. Open the project plan into which the file is to be imported.
2. Choose **File→Open.**
3. In the **Open** dialog box, from the **Files of type** drop-down list, select the format of the file you would be importing.
4. Select the desired file you wish to import and click **Open** to display the **Import Wizard.**
5. In the **Import Wizard,** click **Next.**
6. On the **Import Wizard - Data Type** page, select the format of the data you wish to import and click **Next** to import the selected format into the project plan.

 Selecting the **Only Selected Data** option requires that the user map the data to the project plan.

7. On the **Import Wizard - Import Mode** page, select the format in which you wish to import the data and click **Finish** to import the file into a new project plan.

Procedure Reference: Create Custom Import Maps

To create a custom import map:

1. Display the **Open** dialog box.
2. In the **Open** dialog box, select the file that is to be imported and click **Open.**
3. In the **Import Wizard,** click **Next.**
4. If necessary, on the **Import Wizard - Map** page, select **New Map.**
5. Click **Next.**
6. On the **Import Wizard - Import Mode** page, select the format in which you wish to import the data and click **Next.**
7. On the **Import Wizard - Map Options** page, check the type of data—**Tasks, Resources,** or **Assignments**—you want to import and click **Next.**
8. On the **Import Wizard - Data Mapping** page, choose the names of the database fields you want to import and then map them to the corresponding Microsoft Project fields that will receive the imported data.
9. If necessary, click **Next** and save the map.
   a. On the **Import Wizard - End of Map Definition** page, click **Save Map.**
   b. In the **Save Map** dialog box, in the **Map Name** text box, type a name for the custom map.
   c. Click **Save.**
10. Click **Finish** to import the selected file using the custom import map created.

ACTIVITY 1-1
Importing an Excel Task List into a New Project Plan

Data Files:

C:\084603Data\Exchanging Project Information\CSS Task List.xlsx

Before You Begin:

Microsoft Office 2010 is installed on your system.

Scenario:

A colleague of yours is about to go on maternity leave, and you have inherited one of her projects, which is a training manual about Cascading Style Sheets (CSS). She has provided you with an Excel file containing a basic task list. Currently, it only contains task names and some of her notes. You now have to create a project plan that includes this information.

---

1. Display the **Import Wizard.**

    a. Choose **File→Open,** and in the **Open** dialog box, from the **File type** drop-down list, select **Excel Workbook (*.xlsx).**

    b. Navigate to the C:\084603Data\Exchanging Project Information folder.

    c. Select the **CSS Task List.xlsx** file and click **Open** to display the **Import Wizard.**

---

2. Import the task list in the Excel file to a new project plan.

    a. In the **Import Wizard,** click **Next.**

    b. On the **Import Wizard - Map** page, verify that **New map** is selected and click **Next.**

    c. On the **Import Wizard - Import Mode** page, verify that **As a new project** is selected and click **Next.**

    d. On the **Import Wizard - Map Options** page, check the **Tasks** check box and click **Next.**

    e. On the **Import Wizard - Task Mapping** page, from the **Source worksheet name** drop-down list, select **Sheet1** and click **Finish.**

    f. Observe that the task list is imported into the project plan.

    g. Save the file as *My CSS Task List.mpp* in the Exchanging Project Information folder.

ACTIVITY 1-2
Creating a Custom Import Map

Data Files:

C:\084603Data\Exchanging Project Information\Teams.mdb

Before You Begin:

1. The My CSS Task List.mpp file is open.

2. Ensure that the **Trust Center** settings are configured to allow legacy formats.

↳ *File - options - Trust Ctr - Trust Ctr Settings - legac formot*

Scenario:

You wish to update your project plan with resource information. Your department is divided into four teams, and information about each team is stored in a legacy Access database. Because Project can handle legacy files if the **Trust Center** settings are appropriately set, you decide to go ahead and import the information into your project plan. You will have to map the data manually as you go.

1. Create a new map.

    a. Open the Teams.mdb file in Project to display the **Import Wizard** in the Project interface.

    b. In the **Import Wizard,** click **Next.**

    c. On the **Import Wizard - Map** page, verify that **New map** is selected and click **Next.**

    d. On the **Import Wizard - Import Mode** page, select **Append the data to the active project** and click **Next.**

    e. On the **Import Wizard - Map Options** page, check the **Resources** check box to import resource information and then click **Next.**

    f. On the **Import Wizard - Resource Mapping** page, in the **Map Resources Data** section, from the **Source database table name** drop-down list, select **tblTeam1Resources** to import resource information from the Access database.

    g. In the **Verify or edit how you want to map the data** section, in the **To: Microsoft Office Project Field** column, to the right of the **Resource Name** field, select **(not mapped).**

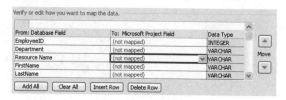

    h. In the entry bar, type *Name* and press **Enter** to map the **Resource Name** field.

2. Save the custom import map.

a.   On the **Import Wizard - Resource Mapping** page, click **Next.**

b.   On the **Import Wizard - End of Map Definition** page, click **Save Map.**

c.   In the **Save Map** dialog box, in the **Map name** text box, type *custom_resource_map* and click **Save** to save the map.

d.   On the **Import Wizard - End of Map Definition** page, click **Finish** to import the resource information.

3.   View the resource information in the project plan.

a.   Display the **Resource Sheet.**

b.   Observe that the resource information is appended to the project plan.

c.   Save the file as *My CSS Project Plan.mpp* in the Exchanging Project Information folder and close the file.

TOPIC B

Export Project Plan Cost Data to an Excel Workbook

In the previous topic, you imported information from other applications into the project plan. Now, you want to share information in the project plan with your colleagues in a more user-friendly format. In this topic, you will export project plan information into an Excel workbook.

One common task you will be performing as a project manager is sharing information with your team members. For example, once you create an internal plan, your team members will want and need to have access to this information. However, because most of your team members do not have Project installed and cannot display the information in Project's native file format, you will need to know how to send the plan in a different format. Rather than re-creating the data in Project, exporting the required information to other applications will minimize your effort and save time. This topic will show you how to more easily prepare and share data with team members by using the export feature.

Export Formats

Exporting is a method of transferring a copy of data from the application in use to a different application. The **Save As** dialog box enables you to export project information with the help of the **Export Wizard.** Project can export all the data, or only selected data from the plan and save it in different file formats such as Excel files, text files, comma-delimited text files, or XML files.

The Export Wizard

The **Export Wizard** allows you to choose the type of data to export—task, resource, or assignment. It reads the Project file and helps you map data from the source file into the destination file. Similar to importing data, once data is exported from a source file to a new destination file format, no connection remains between the two files.

How to Export Project Plan Cost Data to an Excel Workbook

Procedure Reference: Export Project Plan Data to an Excel Workbook Using Existing Maps

To export project plan data to an Excel workbook using existing maps:

1. Open the desired project plan and choose **File→Save As.**

2. In the **Save As** dialog box, from the **Save as type** drop-down list, select **Excel Workbook (*.xlsx).**

3. Click **Save.**

4. In the **Export Wizard,** click **Next.**

5. On the **Export Wizard - Data** page, select the format of the data you want to export.

   - Select **Project Excel Template** to export all the data into the Excel workbook.

   - Select **Selected Data** to export only the data you select into the Excel workbook and click **Next.**

     a. On the **Export Wizard - Map** page, select **Use existing map.**

     b. On the **Export Wizard - Map Selection** page, in the **Choose a map for your data** list box, choose the desired map and click **Next.**

     c. On the **Export Wizard - Map Options** page, select the type of data—**Task, Resource,** or **Assignments**—you want to export and click **Next.**

     d. On the **Export Wizard - Task Mapping** page, choose the names of the database fields in your project you want to export and then map them to the corresponding Excel fields that will receive the exported data. Click **Next** when you have finished.

6. Click **Finish** to export the data.

Procedure Reference: Export Project Plan Data to an Excel Workbook Using Custom Maps

To export project plan data to an Excel workbook using custom maps:

1. Display the **Export Wizard.**

2. In the **Export Wizard,** click **Next.**

3. On the **Export Wizard - Data** page, select **Selected Data** to export specific information and click **Next.**

4. On the **Export Wizard - Map** page, select **New map.**

5. On the **Export Wizard - Map Options** page, select the type of data to export and click **Next.**

6. On the **Export Wizard - {Data} Mapping** page, map the fields as desired.

7. If necessary, click **Next** and save the map.

8. Click **Finish** to export the selected file using the custom export map created.

ACTIVITY 1-3
Exporting Project Plan Cost Data to an Excel File

Data Files:

C:\084603Data\Exchanging Project Information\CSS Book.mpp

Scenario:

Steve, a colleague from the Accounting department, needs to know what the anticipated total cost will be for developing the Cascading Style Sheets training manual. In addition, he needs the total cost broken down by individual tasks; he needs this information by tomorrow. You offer to send him the project plan file through email, so that he can get the required information from the plan himself. However, he quickly replies that he does not have Project on his system, and what he really needs is the cost data in an Excel workbook to enable him run some calculations on it before adding it to the next quarter's budget.

1. Display the cost table in the **Task Sheet** view.

   a. Navigate to the C:\084603Data\Exchanging Project Information folder and open the CSS Book.mpp file.

   b. On the Ribbon, click the **View** tab.

   c. In the **Data** group, click the **Tables** list box, and then click **Cost.**

2. Display the **Export Wizard.**

   a. Choose **File→Save As.**

   b. In the **Save As** dialog box, from the **Save as type** drop-down list, select **Excel Workbook (*.xlsx).**

   c. In the **File name** text box, type *My CSS Task Book*

   d. If necessary, navigate to the C:\084603Data\Exchanging Project Information folder.

   e. Click **Save** to start the **Export Wizard.**

3. Export the plan's cost data into an Excel workbook.

   a. In the **Export Wizard,** click **Next.**

   b. On the **Export Wizard - Data** page, verify that **Selected Data** is selected and click **Next.**

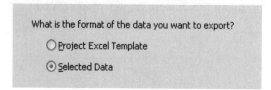

   c. On the **Export Wizard - Map** page, select **Use existing map** and click **Next.**

d. On the **Export Wizard - Map Selection** page, in the **Choose a map for your data** list box, select **Cost data by task** to use it as the export map and then click **Next.**

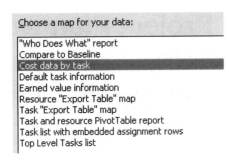

Choose a map for your data:

"Who Does What" report
Compare to Baseline
Cost data by task
Default task information
Earned value information
Resource "Export Table" map
Task "Export Table" map
Task and resource PivotTable report
Task list with embedded assignment rows
Top Level Tasks list

e. On the **Export Wizard - Map Options** page, in the **Select the types of data you want to export** section, verify that the **Tasks** and **Export includes headers** check boxes are checked and click **Next.**

f. On the **Export Wizard - Task Mapping** page, click **Finish** to accept the default field mappings. Note that the default data type is **Text.**

g. Save the file as *My CSS Book.mpp* and close it.

4. View the exported data in the Excel workbook.

a. Choose **Start→All Programs→Microsoft Office→Microsoft Excel 2010.**

b. From the C:\084603Data\Exchanging Project Information folder, open the My CSS Task Book.xlsx file.

c. Observe that the exported data is available as text in the Excel workbook.

d. If necessary, adjust the column widths to display all the exported data.

e. Save the file and close it.

TOPIC C

Copy a Picture of the Project Plan Information

In the previous topic, you exported project information to an Excel workbook. However, you may want to present it in a graphical manner, such as a picture of a Gantt chart or a table in your presentations and reports. In this topic, you will copy a picture of the project plan information into a Word document.

By taking pictures of your project plan, you can include project plan details in a wider variety of applications. So, even though people may not have access to Project or one of the applications that can access exported data, you can still present and share project information in the form of a picture. You can take a snapshot of any project plan view and either paste it into an open file that can display pictures, such as a PowerPoint slide show, or save it as a graphic file that you can attach to an email or store in a folder on your computer.

The Copy Picture Function

You can capture an image of the project plan as a noneditable picture using the **Copy Picture** dialog box. The **Copy Picture** dialog box provides various options to set the way in which the image is rendered or copied. The copied picture can be pasted into Visio, Word, Excel, or PowerPoint, as well as into an email that is being drafted.

The Copy Picture to Office Wizard

In Project 2007, you could also capture an image of the project plan as a noneditable picture using the **Copy Picture to Office Wizard.** The **Copy Picture to Office Wizard** provided additional functionality by automatically pasting the picture into an application of the user's choice. This feature was discontinued in Project 2010.

The Copy Picture Dialog Box

You can display the **Copy Picture** dialog box by clicking the **Copy Picture** button. This dialog box provides various options that help you copy a picture of the project plan.

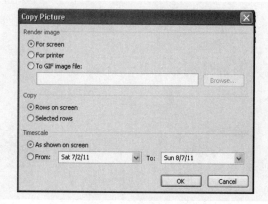

Figure 1-2: The Copy Picture dialog box with options to copy the project plan as a picture.

Section	Enables You To
Render image	Decide on the output format in which the picture is to be copied. The user can select either the **For Screen** or **For Printer** option, depending on whether the image has to appear on screen or in print. To save the picture as a file that can be used on a web page, the user can select the **To GIF image file** option.
Copy	Specify the rows to be included in the picture. The user can include the selected rows, or all the rows on screen.
Timescale	Determine the time range during which the project information is to be copied. The user can either include the dates displayed on the screen, or specify a specific time range.

How to Copy a Picture of the Project Plan Information

Procedure Reference: Copy a Picture of the Project Plan Information

To copy a picture of the project plan information using the **Copy Picture** dialog box:

1. If necessary, modify the position of the columns and charts in the current project plan view.

2. On the Ribbon, on the **Task** tab, in the clipboard group, choose **Copy→Copy Picture.**

3. In the **Copy Picture** dialog box, in the **Render image** section, set the appropriate render options.

4. In the **Copy** section, select whether you want to include all the rows, or just the selected ones.

5. If necessary, in the **Timescale** section, select a time scale.

6. Click **OK.**

7. Launch the desired application, such as PowerPoint, Word, or Visio, and open the document that will receive the picture.

8. Place the insertion point in the desired location and paste the copied picture.

ACTIVITY 1-4

Copying a Picture of the Gantt Chart View into a Word Document

Data Files:

C:\084603Data\Exchanging Project Information\CSS Book.mpp

Scenario:

You are to email a status report to one of your project's key stakeholders. You decide that the best way to provide her the information is to create a Word document with a picture of the project plan in it.

---

1. Rearrange the **Gantt Chart** view to display only the **Task Name** column and the **Gantt** chart.

   a. Open the CSS Book.mpp file.

   b. If necessary, adjust the **Divider** bar so that only the **Task Name** column is visible in the **Entry** table.

   c. Use the vertical and horizontal scroll bars, as well as the zoom slider, to view all the tasks in the **Gantt** chart.

---

2. Copy a picture of the **Gantt Chart.**

   a. On the Ribbon, on the **Task** tab, in the clipboard group, choose **Copy→Copy Picture.**

   b. In the **Copy Picture** dialog box, in the **Render image** section, verify that **For screen** is selected.

   c. In the **Copy** section, verify that **Rows on screen** is selected.

d. In the **Timescale** section, verify that **As shown on screen** is selected and that the date range is approximately mid-July to mid-September, and click **OK.**

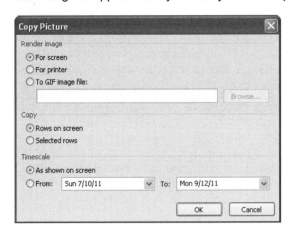

3. Load Microsoft Word and paste the image into a new document.

   a. Open Microsoft Word 2010.

   b. In the new Word document, choose **Paste.**

   c. Verify that the **Gantt** chart has been inserted into the Word file as an image.

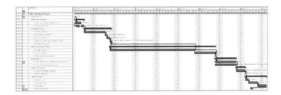

   d. Close Microsoft Word without saving the document.

   e. Close CSS Book.mpp without saving.

Lesson 1 Follow-up

In this lesson, you exchanged project information with other applications by importing task and resource information, exporting task information, and copying a picture of the **Gantt Chart** view. By exchanging project data with other applications, you can save the time that you otherwise have to spend in re-creating the data in the other applications. Also, it helps you share information with your team members in an effective manner.

1. **On your job, what types of business documents will you frequently import into a project plan?**

2. **Why might you want to save project plan information in applications other than Project?**

2 Updating a Project Plan

Lesson Time: 2 hour(s)

Lesson Objectives:

In this lesson, you will update a project plan.

You will:

- Enter task progress.
- Enter overtime work in a project plan.
- Edit a task.
- Reschedule a task.
- Filter tasks in a project plan.
- Set an interim plan for a project plan.
- Create a custom table.
- Create a custom field.

Introduction

In the previous lesson, you exchanged basic information between Project and other applications. As your project enters the Project Implementation phase, the project plan will have to be updated with more specialized and customized values. In this lesson, you will update your project plan.

Updating your project plan helps you maintain effective control over a project. By constantly updating and continuously monitoring a project's progress throughout the Project Implementation phase of its life cycle, you will be able to identify potential problems as they arise. At the very least, you would be better prepared to take appropriate measures to get the project plan back on track if a problem should occur. Remember, you are responsible for steering the project to completion on time and within the stipulated budget despite any problem or challenge that might crop up.

TOPIC A
Enter Task Progress

The Project Implementation phase has commenced, and your project is underway. As work progresses, it is necessary to enter task progress in the project plan. In this topic, you will enter task progress information and view task progress to determine if your project and its tasks are on schedule.

Entering task progress information ensures that your project plan accurately represents your project. This is necessary to compare actual task progress to baseline information. Such a comparison allows you to identify whether a project plan is on schedule. It also helps ensure that you have the necessary information to make in-progress adjustments to the remaining tasks, so that you can keep the actual values as close to the baseline schedule as possible. Keep in mind that just because a plan is progressing, it is not necessarily progressing according to schedule. If you don't keep an eye on both actual progress and the project plan's baseline schedule, you may be in for an unpleasant surprise at the end of a project plan.

The Status Date

The *status date* is a date that is used to check a project's status at a particular point in time. Typically, it is used to enter or view progress information on a date in the past, or used for forecasting. It can be specified on the **Project** tab on the Ribbon. By default, the current date is used as the status date.

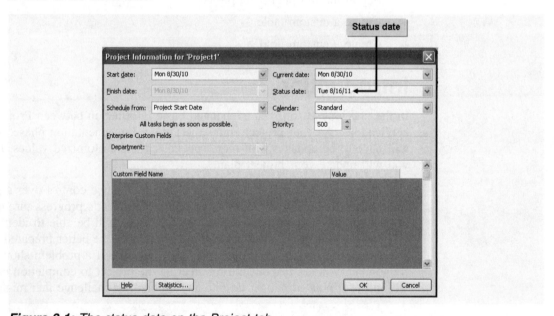

Figure 2-1: The status date on the Project tab.

Gridlines

Gridlines are lines displayed in the **Gantt Chart** and **Tracking Gantt** views. By default, they are displayed for every Sunday and the current date. A gridline can be displayed for the status date if required through the **Gridlines** dialog box. To access the **Gridlines** dialog box, right-click in the **Gantt** chart area and choose **Gridlines** from the shortcut menu.

Progress Bars and Lines

Progress bars are thick black lines that get displayed inside the taskbars in the **Gantt Chart** view, indicating how much of a task has been completed. A *progress line* is a line drawn in the chart portion of a view on either the status date or the current date. A progress line peaks on any **Gantt** bar that intersects with it; if a progress line peaks to the right, it means that a task is ahead of schedule, and if it peaks to the left, the task is behind schedule.

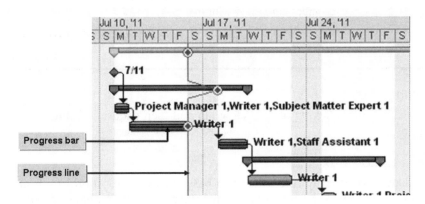

Figure 2-2: *Progress bars and lines in the Gantt chart.*

Multiple Progress Lines

You can display multiple progress lines at recurring intervals if desired. They are displayed in the **Gantt** chart from the project's start date up to the status date, or up to the current date if the status date is not set. They can be set to recur at daily, weekly, or monthly intervals.

Task Status Information

Current task status can be seen from the **Status Indicator** column as well as the **Status** column. These columns can be inserted into a view. The **Status Indicator** column displays an icon indicating completed tasks, tasks on schedule, and late tasks, on the status date. No icon is displayed for tasks scheduled to start after the status date. The **Status** column tells you whether a task is complete, late, on schedule, or a future task on the status date. It is a convenient textual alternative to the **Status Indicator** column. If a status date is not set, the current date is used.

The Tracking Table

The **Tracking** table is a view that allows you to track task progress. The table's default column headers offer several options to gather and display tracking-related information.

Column Header	Description
Act. Start	Actual Start. The date that a task actually began.
Act. Finish	Actual Finish. The date that a task was actually completed.
% Comp	Percent Completed. The present status of a task, expressed as a percent of the task's duration.
Phys % Comp	Physical Percent Completed. A percent complete value that can also be used to help calculate budgeted cost of work performed.

Column Header	Description
Act. Dur	Actual Duration. The length of actual working time for the task up to this point.
Rem. Dur	Remaining Duration. The amount of time necessary to complete the task.
Act. Cost	Actual Cost. The cost of the work that has been completed by resources connected with that task.
Act. Work	Actual Work. The amount of work that has already been completed by resources assigned to the tasks.

Accessing the Tracking Table

The **Tracking** table is available by clicking on the **View** tab and then choosing **Tables→ Tracking** in the **Data** group.

The Project Statistics Dialog Box

The **Project Statistics** dialog box displays the actual and baseline values for a project. It also displays the projected values based on the actual values for the project. It can be accessed from the Backstage view by choosing **Project Information→Project Statistics,** or by clicking **Project Information** on the **Project** tab, and then clicking **Statistics.**

Schedule Tracking Options

Microsoft Project 2010 provides you with many tools to update selected tasks and illustrate their progress.

Tool	Description
Percentage Complete	Updates the actual work for selected tasks as the specified percentage complete. Users can choose 0%, 25%, 50%, 75%, or 100%. These buttons are located on the **Task** tab in the **Schedule** group.
Mark on Track	Allows you to either mark the task as **On Track,** or launch the **Update Tasks** dialog box. This tool is available on the **Tasks** tab in the **Schedule** group.
Move Task	Allows you to move a task forward, move a task backward, or reschedule a task. This option is available on the **Tasks** tab in the **Tasks** group.
Add Progress Line	Allows you to add progress lines by clicking in the **Gantt** chart.
Update Project	Launches the **Update Project** dialog box. This dialog box has options for updating completed work, or rescheduling uncompleted work.
Update Tasks	Launches the **Update Tasks** dialog box. This dialog box has options for setting the percentage of the task that has been completed, the task's actual and remaining durations, and the task's actual start and finish dates. This tool is available on the **Tasks** tab in the **Schedule** group, and is accessed by clicking the **Mark on Track** drop-down button.

The Tracking Gantt Chart

The **Tracking Gantt** chart is displayed in the **Tracking Gantt** view. It displays the percentage of work completed per task. Demarcation of noncritical taskbars and shading of critical taskbars also indicate the amount of work completed. **Gantt** bars indicating progress for summary tasks and the project summary task are also visible. Actual progress can be compared to planned progress as **Gantt** bars corresponding to baseline start and finish dates are displayed.

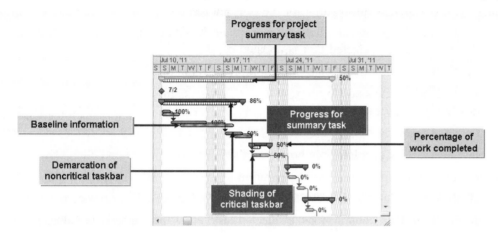

Figure 2-3: Progress information in the Tracking Gantt chart.

Bar Styles and Text Styles

By right-clicking in the **Gantt** chart area, you can choose **Bar Styles,** and the **Bar Styles** dialog box loads. From here, you can select options for both the text and the bars displayed in the **Gantt Chart,** including color, shape, pattern, and location.

The Variance Table

The **Variance** table allows you to check whether your project is on track. The **Start** and **Finish** columns display actual dates for tasks that have started and projected dates for those that have not, respectively. The **Baseline Start** and **Baseline Finish** columns display the planned start and finish dates. The **Start Var** and **Finish Var** columns show the difference between the actual and baseline dates. Negative numbers indicate tasks that are ahead of schedule, whereas positive numbers indicate tasks that are behind schedule. The **Variance** table is accessed on the Ribbon by clicking the **View** tab and then clicking **Tables** in the **Data** group.

The Date, Cost, and Work Variances

Some common variances that project managers check are the date, cost, and work variances. However, they are not available in the **Variance** table by default. To access these variances:

- For Date or Duration variance, add a Duration Variance column.

- For Cost variance, choose **Tables→Cost.**

- For Work variance, choose **Tables→Work.**

How to Enter Task Progress

Procedure Reference: Enter Task Progress Information

To enter task progress information:

1. On the **View** tab, choose **Tables→Tracking** to display the **Tracking** table.

2. In the **Tracking** table, select the task that is to be updated.

3. Enter the task progress information for the selected task.

   - On the **Tracking** toolbar, click the appropriate **% Complete** button and observe how the values for the selected task is updated or;

   - In the **% Comp** column, enter the appropriate value or;

   - In the **Update Tasks** dialog box, enter task progress information.

     a. On the **Tracking** toolbar, click the **Update Tasks** button to launch the **Update Tasks** dialog box.

     b. In the **% Complete** spin box, type the appropriate value and click **OK.**

4. If necessary, select a task and alter its duration.

   a. If necessary, click the **0% Complete** button to mark the task as 0% complete.

   b. In the **Rem. Dur** column, for the selected task, enter the appropriate value.

   c. If necessary, in the **% Comp** column of the task, enter the original value so that the **Act. Dur** column is updated as desired.

5. If desired, view task progress using progress bars.

   a. Display the **Gantt Chart** view.

   b. In the **Gantt** chart, move the mouse pointer over a progress bar for an in-progress task to display progress information as a screentip.

Procedure Reference: Display Progress Lines in the Tracking Gantt View

To display progress lines in the **Tracking Gantt** view:

1. In the **Project Information** dialog box, set the status date.

   - In the **Status date** text box, type an appropriate date and click **OK** or;

   - From the **Status date** drop-down list, select an appropriate date and click **OK.**

2. Display the **Tracking Gantt** view.

 Progress lines can be displayed in any view that has a chart.

3. In the **Tracking Gantt** chart, right-click and choose **Progress Lines** to display the **Progress Lines** dialog box.

4. Check the **Always display current progress line** check box and if necessary, select **At project status date.**

5. Click **OK** to display a progress line in the **Tracking Gantt** chart on the status date.

6. If necessary, remove the progress line.

   a. Display the **Progress Lines** dialog box.

   b. Uncheck the **Always display current progress line** check box and click **OK.**

Procedure Reference: Insert the Status Indicator Column

To insert the **Status Indicator** column:

1. Choose **Insert→Column** to display the **Column Definition** dialog box.
2. From the **Field name** drop-down list, select **Status Indicator** and click **OK** to display the **Status Indicator** column in the current view.

 When a column is inserted into a view, it is inserted to the left of the currently selected column. By default, the first column in a view is selected.

3. If necessary, reposition the **Status Indicator** column in the current view.
    a. Move the mouse pointer over the **Status Indicator** column heading and click to select it.
    b. Click the selected column and drag it to the desired location in the view.
4. If necessary, remove the **Status Indicator** column from the current view.
    a. Select the **Status Indicator** column.
    b. Press **Delete**.

The Status Indicator in Other Views

The **Status Indicator** column can also be displayed in a custom view by clicking the **Check the progress of the project** link in the **Track** pane of the **Project Guide.** However, this custom view is rather limited when compared to other tables, such as **Tracking** and **Variance,** which provide far more detailed task progress information. Inserting the **Status Indicator** column into one of these tables will provide better insight into task progress.

ACTIVITY 2-1
Entering Task Progress in a Project Plan

Data Files:

C:\084603Data\Updating a Project Plan\CSS Week1.mpp

Scenario:

The Cascading Style Sheet (CSS) Training Manual project has been underway for a week now. It is now Monday morning, 7/18/11, and you have been notified of the progress made on tasks. The following progress has been made.

1. Task 1—Start Book started on time and can be marked as 100% complete.

2. Task 3—Interview Subject Matter Expert has been completed, but lasted only one day instead of two.

3. Task 4—Investigate the Software is completed as the writer has completed 32 hours of work on it.

You need to enter this task progress information in your project plan. Having entered this task progress information, it would also be a good idea to determine if your project is on schedule at the end of the first week.

---

1. Set the status date as 7/15/11 in the **Project Information** dialog box.

   a. From the C:\084603Data\Updating a Project Plan folder, open the CSS Week1.mpp file.

   b. Display the **Project Information** dialog box.

   c. From the **Status date** drop-down list, select **7/15/11** and click **OK.**

---

2. Enter the task progress information for tasks 1, 3, and 4.

   a. Switch to the **View** tab and display the **Tracking** table.

   b. In the **% Comp** column for task 1, enter *100* to mark the task as fully complete.

   c. In the **Rem. Dur** column for task 3, enter *1*

   d. Observe the changes highlighted in the **Tracking** table and click the **Task** tab.

			%	%		
CSS Training Ma	Mon 7/11/11	NA	0%	0%	0 days	52 days
1 Start Book	Mon 7/11/11	Mon 7/11/11	100%	0%	0 days	0 days
⊟ 2 Research Phas	NA	NA	0%	0%	0 days	7 days
2.1 Interview S	NA	NA	0%	0%	0 days	1 day

   e. Select task 3.

   f. On the **Task** tab, in the **Schedule** group, click the **100% Complete** button so that task 3 is marked 100% complete in the **% Comp** column.

---

g.   On the **View** tab, display the **Variance** table so that the variance for task 3 and its dependent tasks is visible.

h.   Observe that the finish variance of task 3 has changed. Also, observe that the start and finish variances of task 3's dependent tasks have changed.

i.   Display the **Tracking** table.

j.   In the **Act. Work** column, for task 4, enter *32*

3.   Display progress information from the progress bars.

a.   Display the **Gantt Chart** view.

b.   In the **Gantt** chart, move the mouse pointer over the progress bar for task 3 to display progress information as a screentip.

4.   Display progress lines to determine if your tasks are on schedule on the status date 7/15/11.

a.   Display the **Tracking Gantt** view.

b.   Drag the divide bar to the left to view more of the **Tracking Gantt** chart.

c.   In the **Tracking Gantt** chart, right-click and choose **Progress Lines** to display the **Progress Lines** dialog box.

d.   In the **Current progress line** area, check the **Display** check box, verify that **At project status date** is selected, and click **OK** to display a progress line in the **Tracking Gantt** chart on the status date.

e.   Observe that the progress line peaks to the right indicating that the tasks are ahead of schedule on the status date 7/15/11.

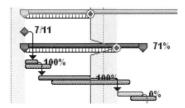

5.   Insert the **Status Indicator** column in the current view.

a.   On the **Format** tab, choose **Insert Column**.

b.   From the drop-down list, select **Status Indicator** to display the **Status Indicator** column.

c.   Move the mouse pointer over the **Status Indicator** column's heading and click to select it.

d.   Click the selected **Status Indicator** column's heading and drag the column to the right of the **Task Name** column.

e.   Save the file as *My CSS Week1.mpp* and close it.

TOPIC B
Enter Overtime Work

In the previous topic, you entered task progress information. As tasks progress, it may be necessary for employees to work overtime, and the project plan should be updated to reflect this. In this topic, you will enter overtime work.

Sometimes, the allocated time frame for tasks is not sufficient and employees have to put in extra hours outside regular working times to meet deadlines. This overtime work affects a project plan in terms of effort—person-hours worked on tasks, and costs of tasks. Having accurate actual values affects decision making to keep the project within the fixed budget. Therefore, to maintain an up-to-date, accurate project plan, overtime work should be entered in the project plan.

Overtime Work

Definition:

Overtime work is the extra hours of work put in by employees outside of regular working hours. It is entered in the **Overtime Work** column only for work resources, and not for material and cost resources. However, entering hours of overtime work merely allots some of the total hours assigned for task completion as overtime work. It does not increase the total number of hours assigned for task completion. Overtime work cannot be entered for completed tasks.

Example:

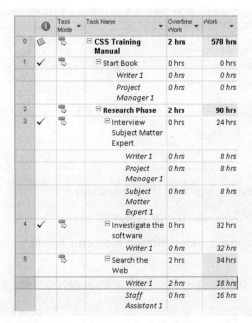

		Task Mode	Task Name	Overtime Work	Work
0			⊟ **CSS Training Manual**	**2 hrs**	**578 hrs**
1	✓		⊟ Start Book	0 hrs	0 hrs
			Writer 1	0 hrs	0 hrs
			Project Manager 1	0 hrs	0 hrs
2			⊟ **Research Phase**	**2 hrs**	**90 hrs**
3	✓		⊟ Interview Subject Matter Expert	0 hrs	24 hrs
			Writer 1	0 hrs	8 hrs
			Project Manager 1	0 hrs	8 hrs
			Subject Matter Expert 1	0 hrs	8 hrs
4	✓		⊟ Investigate the software	0 hrs	32 hrs
			Writer 1	0 hrs	32 hrs
5			⊟ Search the Web	2 hrs	34 hrs
			Writer 1	2 hrs	18 hrs
			Staff Assistant 1	0 hrs	16 hrs

Figure 2-4: The Overtime Work column in a project plan.

 When the **Work** column contains 0 hours, entering hours of overtime work in the **Overtime Work** column updates the **Work** column with the same number of hours.

How to Enter Overtime Work

Procedure Reference: Enter Overtime Work

To enter overtime work:

1. Display all the columns of the **Work** table.

 The **Usage** table is the default table in the **Task Usage** view. It is also useful for entering overtime work because it displays the start and finish dates for tasks, task durations, and hours worked.

2. Adjust the table size until the **Add New Column** column appears.

3. Click the **Add New Column** column and scroll down to select **Overtime Work.**

4. In the **Overtime Work** column, for the required task, enter the appropriate value for the resource that has worked overtime.

5. In the **Work** column, for the required resource, increase the value by the number of hours in the **Overtime Work** column and press **Enter.**

6. Select the task for which the resource has worked overtime.

7. On the **Task** tab on the Ribbon, click the **100% Complete** button so that the selected task is marked 100% in the **% W. Comp** column.

ACTIVITY 2-2
Entering Overtime Work

Data Files:

C:\084603Data\Updating a Project Plan\CSS Week2.mpp

Scenario:

The CSS Training Manual project is progressing and task 5—Search the Web, has been completed on time. However, Writer 1 informs you that she had to work two hours overtime in order to finish the task. As the project manager, you need to update the project plan to reflect this.

---

1. Insert the **Overtime Work** column in the **Work** table of the **Task Usage** view.

   a. From the C:\084603Data\Updating a Project Plan folder, open the CSS Week2.mpp file.

   b. Click the **View** tab on the Ribbon, switch to the **Task Usage** view, and display the **Work** table.

   c. Drag the divider bar to display all the columns of the **Work** table.

   d. Select the **Work** column.

   e. Click the **Format** tab on the Ribbon, click **Insert Column** in the **Columns** group, and scroll down to select **Overtime Work.**

---

2. Mark task 5 as 100% complete with two hours of overtime work by Writer 1.

   a. In the **Overtime Work** column, for Writer 1 working on task 5, enter *2*

   b. Observe that the value in the **Work** column for Writer 1 does not increase. This is because two hours out of the total hours in the **Work** column is set as overtime work.

   c. In the **Work** column, for Writer 1 working on task 5, enter *18* to increase the total hours worked.

   d. Click the exclamation point drop-down and select **Increase the hours the resource works per day, so the duration stays the same.**

   e. Observe the changes highlighted in the **Work** table.

   f. Select task 5 and mark it as 100% complete.

   g. Save the file as *My CSS Week2.mpp* and close it.

TOPIC C
Edit Tasks

Task progress information, including overtime work, has been entered in the project plan. However, unexpected events may interrupt work on a task. In this topic, you will edit tasks to account for an unexpected interruption of work.

While your project is in progress, unexpected events can interrupt work on tasks. Weather conditions, power outages, changes in task priorities, and health issues of employees are a few typical examples. In such cases, the project plan should be updated to account for any interruption of work, or changes requested.

Split Tasks

When a task's schedule is interrupted by an unexpected event such as adverse weather conditions or a power outage, the task should be split to account for the interruption. By default, an interruption of one day is inserted in the project plan. The duration of interruption can be increased or decreased by clicking and dragging the right segment of a split task. A task can be split multiple times, if required, in any view that contains a chart.

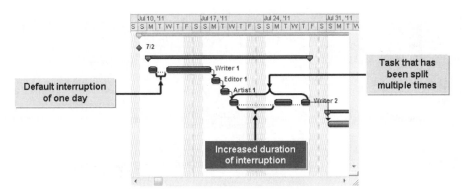

Figure 2-5: *Gantt chart containing taskbars that have been split.*

Active/Inactive Tasks

Project 2010 offers a new feature that allows you to designate certain tasks as inactive. An *inactive task* is a task that is cut from the project timeline, yet does not disappear from the project as a whole. Inactive tasks allow you retain records of tasks that get cut as a project changes scope, and allows you to insert a few "what if" scenarios into an active project plan in an effort to discover the best possible method of tackling a problem. Inactive tasks appear on the Task Sheet as crossed-out gray text, and in the **Gantt Chart** view, they appear as bars filled with solid white.

Inactive Task Availability in Project 2010

The Inactive Task feature is not available in all versions of Microsoft Project. It is available only in Project 2010 Professional (not Standard), and is also not available while in Project 2007 compatibility mode.

Canceling an Unneeded Task

Setting a task to inactive is one way to safely cancel a task that is no longer needed. Another method of doing this is zeroing out the remaining work. Zeroing out remaining work would occur if a resource leaves the company and you need to reassign his work to someone else; his work can be zeroed out and the tasks reassigned to a new resource. This would also be useful should a task no longer be required in order to reach a milestone.

Placeholder Tasks

Definition:

A *placeholder task* is a manually created task that you can enter into your project even if it does not have much information associated with it. A placeholder task can be a task name only, or it can include any combination of start date, finish date, and duration; the rest can be defined as it becomes known. Placeholder tasks serve as reminders to yourself, and allow a project schedule to be created despite some aspect of a task not being fully known. Tasks without start dates are automatically treated as placeholder tasks.

Example:

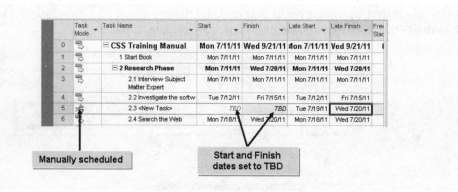

Figure 2-6: *A task without a start date is automatically treated as a placeholder.*

How to Edit Tasks

Procedure Reference: Split a Task

To split a task:

1. Display the split-task cursor by choosing the **Task** tab, then choosing **Split Task.**
2. In the **Gantt** chart, place the split-task cursor over the taskbar you want to split.
3. Move the split-task cursor along the taskbar, until you see the date on which the task is to be split in the screentip.
4. Click to split the taskbar with an interruption of one day.
5. If necessary, alter the duration of the interruption.
   a. In the **Gantt** chart, place the mouse pointer over the right segment of the split taskbar so that the mouse pointer changes to a four-pointed arrow.
   b. Drag the right segment of the task to the right to increase the duration of the interruption, or to the left to shorten the interruption's duration, or remove the split as required.

Procedure Reference: Inactivate a Task

To inactivate a task:

1. Ensure that the task to be inactivated is selected.
2. Inactivate the task.
   - Click the **Task** tab on the Ribbon, and in the **Schedule** group, click **Inactivate** or;
   - Right-click the task and select **Inactivate Task** or;
   - If necessary, add the **Active** column to your project plan and set the value to **No** or;
   - On the **Task** tab of the Ribbon, from the **Information** button in the **Properties** group, click **General** and check the **Inactive** check box.

Procedure Reference: Activate a Task

To activate a task:

1. Ensure that the task to be activated is selected.
2. Activate the task.
   - Click the **Task** tab on the Ribbon, and in the **Schedule** group, click **Activate** or;
   - Right-click the task and select **Activate Task** or;
   - If necessary, add the **Active** column to your project plan and set the value to **Yes** or;
   - On the **Task** tab of the Ribbon, from the **Information** button in the **Properties** group, click **General** and uncheck **Inactive.**

ACTIVITY 2-3
Splitting a Task

Data Files:

C:\084603Data\Updating a Project Plan\CSS Week3.mpp

Scenario:

It is Tuesday, 7/25/11; another week has gone by, and task progress information has been submitted by resources working on the CSS Training Manual project. The writer assigned to task 7—Create Outline, reported that although she completed the task, it was not finished on schedule. She started the 3-day task on Wednesday as planned, but due to the severe thunderstorm on Thursday night and a city-wide power outage the next day, the office was closed on Friday. So, the task could not be completed until Monday. As a project manager, you need to account for the interruption of work in the project plan.

1. In the **Gantt Chart** view, mark task 7 as 100% complete.

    a. From the C:\084603Data\Updating a Project Plan folder, open the CSS Week3.mpp file.

    b. In the **Gantt Chart** view, select task 7.

    c. On the **Task** tab, click the **100% Complete** button to display a completed indicator, ✓ in the **Indicators** column for task 7.

    d. Observe that in the **Gantt** chart, a progress bar is drawn on the taskbar for task 7.

2. Split task 7 on 7/22/11 to insert an interruption of three days.

    a. On the **Task** tab, click the **Split Task** button, 🎬 to display the split-task cursor.

    b. In the **Gantt** chart, move the split-task cursor along the taskbar for task 7 until the date 7/22/11 is displayed in the screentip and click to split the taskbar.

    c. Observe that an interruption of three days is inserted.

3. **When task 7 is split, why is an interruption of three days inserted instead of the default one day?**

    a) Due to a constraint on task 7

    b) Due to the task relationship of task 7 and task 8

    c) Due to the fact that task 7 was split on a Friday

    d) Due to resource limitations for task 7

4. Edit the note for task 7 to mention the reason for splitting the task.

    a.   Launch the **Task Information** dialog box.

    b.   On the **Notes** page, in the **Notes** text area, type *Work interrupted on 7/22/11 due to city-wide power outage* and click **OK.**

    c.   In the **Indicators** column, move the mouse pointer over the note for task 7 to view the edited note's content in the screentip.

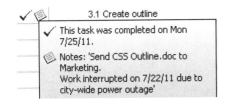

    d.   Save the file as *My CSS Week3.mpp* and close it.

TOPIC D
Reschedule a Task

In the previous topic, you edited a task in your project plan. When work is interrupted and you need to split or otherwise edit a task, you may also want to specify the date on which uncompleted work should resume. In this topic, you will reschedule a task to resume on a specified date.

Situations may arise where an employee is unable to complete work on a task as scheduled, perhaps due to a higher-priority assignment or for personal reasons. In such cases, other resources may be unavailable to complete the work, or you may wish to retain the same employee on the task in light of her qualifications, skill level, or familiarity with the task. Project helps you handle such unavoidable delays by rescheduling the task to resume on a date you specify with the same employee. This avoids rushing the task to completion, requiring unreasonable work hours, and assigning unqualified resources to meet the deadline.

How to Reschedule a Task

Procedure Reference: Reschedule a Task

To reschedule a task:

1. In the **Gantt Chart** view, select the task that is to be rescheduled.
2. If necessary, on the **Task** tab on the Ribbon, click the appropriate **% Complete** button, so that a progress bar indicating partial completion is drawn on the selected task's taskbar.
3. If necessary, in the **Editing** group, click the **Scroll to Task** button to display the selected task's taskbar in the **Gantt** chart.
4. Choose **Project→Update Project** to display the **Update Project** dialog box.
5. Select **Reschedule uncompleted work to start after** and specify the appropriate date on which uncompleted work should resume.

    *   In the **Reschedule uncompleted work to start after** text box, type the appropriate date or;
    *   From the **Reschedule uncompleted work to start after** drop-down list, select the appropriate date.
6. Select **Selected tasks** and click **OK** to reschedule the selected task.

ACTIVITY 2-4
Rescheduling a Task

Data Files:

C:\084603Data\Updating a Project Plan\CSS Week10.mpp

Scenario:

It is now the second week of September. Editor 1 is unavailable for work on Thursday and Friday due to a family emergency and he has completed only 50% of task 15—Check Grammar, Spelling, and Proofread. Because no one else is available to work on the task, you need to reschedule the remaining work to resume when he returns on Monday 9/19/11.

---

1. Mark task 15 as 50% complete.

   a. From the C:\084603Data\Updating a Project Plan folder, open the CSS Week10.mpp file.

   b. In the **Gantt Chart** view, select task 15.

   c. On the **Task** tab of the Ribbon, in the **Schedule** group, click the **50% Complete** button.

   d. On the **Task** tab of the Ribbon, in the **Editing** group, click the **Scroll to Task** button to display the selected task's taskbar in the **Gantt** chart.

   e. Observe that in the **Gantt** chart, a progress bar is drawn on the taskbar for task 15 to indicate 50% completion.

---

2. Reschedule task 15 so that its uncompleted work resumes on 9/19/11.

   a. Click the **Project** tab of the Ribbon, and in the **Status** group, click **Update Project** to display the **Update Project** dialog box.

   b. Select **Reschedule uncompleted work to start after,** and from the **Reschedule uncompleted work to start after** drop-down list, select **9/16/11.**

   c. Select **Selected tasks** and click **OK.**

   d. Observe how the rescheduled task's taskbar changes in the **Gantt Chart** view.

---

3. Add a note to task 15 stating the reason for rescheduling it.

   a. Double-click task 15 to launch the **Task Information** dialog box.

   b. If necessary, select the **Notes** tab.

c.   On the **Notes** page, in the **Notes** text area, type *Task rescheduled because Editor 1 was unavailable on 9/15/11 and 9/16/11 due to family emergency* and click **OK** to display a note in the **Indicators** column.

d.   Save the file as *My CSS Week10.mpp* and close it.

TOPIC E
Filter Tasks

In the previous topic, you rescheduled a task due to circumstances beyond your control. Now, you need to check whether this action has delayed the project's schedule. One way to learn that information is through filtering tasks. In this topic, you will filter tasks to display only those that meet given criteria, such as those that are behind the schedule.

Once a project is underway, you have to periodically identify tasks and resources based on certain criteria and take action accordingly. Hunting through Project's different tables to find such information is a tedious, time-consuming, and error-prone process. In Project, filters allow you to view only the information you are interested in, while hiding information that does not fit the selection criteria. Once you retrieve the necessary information, you can proceed with taking corrective action to fix any problem, instead of wasting time searching for the source of the problem.

Filters

Definition:

In Project, a *filter* is a tool that controls the display of information based on specified selection criteria. Applying a filter alters the existing view by including or excluding certain project information based on the selection criteria. It does not result in any permanent change to the project plan. Filters may be predefined, custom, or AutoFilters.

Example:

Start	Finish	Predecessors	Resource Names	Critical
Mon 7/11/11	Thu 9/22/11			Yes
Mon 7/11/11	Mon 7/11/11		Project Manager 1,Writer 1	No
Mon 7/11/11	Tue 7/19/11			No
Mon 7/11/11	Mon 7/11/11	1	Project Manager 1,Writer 1,Subject Matter Expert 1	No
Tue 7/12/11	Fri 7/15/11	3	Writer 1	No
Mon 7/18/11	Tue 7/19/11	4	Writer 1,Staff Assistant 1	No
Wed 7/20/11	Fri 7/29/11			No
Wed 7/20/11	Mon 7/25/11	5	Writer 1	No
Tue 7/26/11	Tue 7/26/11	7	Writer 1,Project Manager 1,Publisher 1	No
Wed 7/27/11	Thu 7/28/11	8	Writer 1,Subject Matter Expert 1	No
Fri 7/29/11	Fri 7/29/11	9	Writer 1	No

Before-no filter applied

Start	Finish	Predecessors	Resource Names	Critical
Mon 7/11/11	Thu 9/22/11			Yes
Tue 9/13/11	Thu 9/15/11			Yes
Tue 9/13/11	Thu 9/15/11	13	Editor 1	Yes
Wed 9/14/11	Thu 9/15/11	15FF	Editor 1,Subject Matter Expert 1	Yes
Fri 9/16/11	Mon 9/19/11			Yes

After-filter applied

Figure 2-7: Applying a filter.

The More Filters Dialog Box

The **More Filters** dialog box provides access to all available filters. It can also be used to edit existing filters and create new filters. It can be accessed on the **View** tab by choosing the **Filter** drop-down list, then **More Filters.**

The Slipping Tasks Filter

The **Slipping Tasks** filter is one of the more commonly used prebuilt filters in Microsoft Project. It is used to identify all the tasks that have not started yet that also have a finish date that is later than the baseline finish date. To apply this filter, go to the **View** tab, and then choose **Filter→More Filters→Slipping Tasks.**

AutoFilters

If you want to filter table data quickly based on column-specific criteria, you can use the AutoFilter feature. This places a column-specific drop-down list of AutoFilters to the right of each column heading. For example, if you want to see tasks scheduled to begin today, you can click the **AutoFilter** button and then select the **Today** value from the **Start** column's **AutoFilter** drop-down list. Any task scheduled to start on the current date will be displayed.

Turning AutoFilter On and Off

To remove the drop-down arrow from the column header, thus disabling the AutoFilter features for your current view, choose the **View** tab, then the **Filter** drop-down list, then **Display AutoFilter.** AutoFilter is enabled by default in Microsoft Project 2010. If AutoFilter is currently applied to a column, a funnel-shaped icon is displayed next to the heading. The status bar will also indicate whether AutoFilters are applied.

AutoFilter Menu Zones

AutoFilter features can now be configured directly from a column header. By clicking the drop-down arrow to the right of a column heading, you can activate the **AutoFilter** menu, which has four zones.

AutoFilter Menu Zone	Description
Sorting	Sorts information alphabetically, numerically, or chronologically.
Group by	Groups information on the field, or according to a field type.
Filters	Selects values to display by selecting criteria.
Checkboxes	Selects values to display by checking or unchecking the check boxes that correspond to information values. This zone is similar to the Filters zone, though not as fast.

Highlighting

Another way to draw attention to specific areas of a project plan is through highlighting. You can either highlight specific cells, or automatically highlight cells if they meet predefined criteria.

How to Filter Tasks

Procedure Reference: Filter Tasks

To filter tasks:

1. On the **View** tab, click the **Filter** drop-down arrow.

2. From the **Filter** drop-down list, select the appropriate filter to display only the tasks that match the filter.

3. If you have selected the **Date Range, Task Range,** or **Using Resource** filters, enter the requested information in the dialog box and click **OK.**

 Changing the table displayed in the current view does not remove a filter or an AutoFilter that has been applied. However, switching to another view, removes any filter or AutoFilter that has been applied.

Procedure Reference: Filter by Using AutoFilters

To filter by using AutoFilters:

1. Click the appropriate column's **AutoFilter** drop-down arrow to display the **AutoFilter** menu.

2. From the **AutoFilter** menu, choose the appropriate **Group by, Sorting, Filters,** or **Checkboxes** filter.

Procedure Reference: Highlight Cells

To highlight a cell or a group of cells:

1. Select the cell or cells that you want to highlight.

2. On the **Task** tab on the Ribbon, in the **Font** group, click the drop-down arrow of **Background Color.**

3. From the drop-down list, select a theme color or a standard color; or you can click **More Colors** to choose from additional colors.

Procedure Reference: Highlight Categories of Cells

To highlight specific categories of cells:

1. On the **Format** tab, in the **Format** group, click **Text Styles.**

2. In the **Text Styles** dialog box, from the **Item to Change** drop-down list, select the category of cells you want to highlight.

3. In the **Text Styles** dialog box, change the other options as appropriate.

4. Click **OK** to save and apply changes.

ACTIVITY 2-5
Filtering Tasks

Data Files:

C:\084603Data\Updating a Project Plan\CSS Week11.mpp

Scenario:

You had to reschedule task 15—Check Grammar, Spelling, and Proofread because Editor 1 was unavailable for a couple of days due to a family emergency. To see the consequences of this action, you need to filter tasks to display only the incompleted ones that now have a date variance from the baseline after rescheduling task 15.

---

1. Check whether the current finish date is greater than the baseline finish date.

    a. From the C:\084603Data\Updating a Project Plan folder, open the CSS Week11.mpp file.

    b. Launch the **Project Statistics** dialog box.

    c. Observe that in the **Finish** column, the current finish date is greater than the baseline finish date and close the dialog box.

Finish
Tue 9/27/11
Thu 9/22/11
NA
2.5d

---

2. Apply the **Incomplete Tasks** filter.

    a. On the **View** tab, in the **Data** group, click the **Filter** drop-down arrow.

    b. From the **Filter** drop-down list, select the **Incomplete Tasks** filter to display only the slipping tasks.

---

3. Display the relevant tasks in the **Variance** table.

    a. Display the **Variance** table.

    b. Observe that the **Incomplete Tasks** filter is still in effect and that only the relevant affected tasks are displayed.

    c. Save the file as *My CSS Week 11.mpp* and close it.

TOPIC F
Set an Interim Plan

So far in this lesson, you have made various updates to a project plan. As the project is about to enter a new phase of implementation, you may want to save a copy of all the current dates at that point for future reference. In this topic, you will set an interim plan.

Each phase or stage of a project plan is of individual significance. It may be useful to save a copy of all the current dates at a particular stage so that they are available for future reference. Once saved, they can also be compared to baseline data, to judge whether the project is proceeding as planned at a specific stage. Interim plans serve this purpose.

Interim Plans

An *interim plan* saves a copy of the current start and finish dates that can be set once a project is underway. It can be set for the entire project or for selected tasks. Up to 10 interim plans can be set; each to signify particular stages or phases of a project plan. Interim plans help you monitor project progress at a particular stage by comparing interim dates to baseline dates. Interim plans can be set even if a baseline is not set. However, they may not be of much use without baseline information for the sake of comparison.

Multiple Interim Plans

In the case of multiple interim plans, you will have to select the interim plan that is to be set or cleared in the **Set Baseline** or the **Clear Baseline** dialog box, respectively. Each interim plan is denoted by the names of a pair of columns. For instance, **Start1/Finish1** is the first interim plan, **Start2/Finish2** corresponds to the second interim plan, and so on. It is up to the user to remember which stage of a project plan each interim plan corresponds to because there is no facility to check the date on which an interim plan was set.

How to Set an Interim Plan

Procedure Reference: Set an Interim Plan for a Project

To set an interim plan for a project:

1. Open the project plan for which baseline data is set.
2. Display the **Set Baseline** dialog box.
3. Select **Set interim plan.**
4. If necessary, from the **Set interim plan** drop-down list, select the appropriate pair of columns corresponding to the interim plan to be set.
5. In the **For** section, if necessary, select **Selected tasks.**
6. If necessary, check the **To all summary tasks** check box so that changes to selected tasks are updated on all summary tasks that the selected tasks fall under.
7. If necessary, check the **From subtasks into selected summary task(s)** check box so that only the selected summary tasks are updated.
8. Click **OK.**
9. Add **Start1** and **Finish1** columns to the plan to view it.

Procedure Reference: Clear an Interim Plan

To clear an interim plan:

1. Display the **Clear Baseline** dialog box.
2. Select **Clear interim plan.**
3. If necessary, from the **Clear interim plan** drop-down list, select the appropriate pair of **Start** and **Finish** columns corresponding to the interim plan to be deleted.
4. Click **OK.**

ACTIVITY 2-6
Setting an Interim Plan for a Project

Data Files:

C:\084603Data\Updating a Project Plan\CSS Week12.mpp

Scenario:

The project is about to enter the Review phase, and the company protocols have been recently revised. The new stipulations require project managers to save a copy of all task start and finish dates prior to each phase of a project. Your reporting manager asks you to set an interim plan for this purpose.

---

1. Check whether a baseline is set for the project plan.

    a. From the C:\084603Data\Updating a Project Plan folder, open the CSS Week12.mpp file.

    b. Display the **Project Statistics** dialog box.

    c. Verify that the **Baseline** rows contain values other than 0 and NA.

    d. Close the **Project Statistics** dialog box.

---

2. Set an interim plan for the project.

    a. Display the **Set Baseline** dialog box.

    b. Select **Set interim plan.**

    c. In the **For** section, verify that **Entire project** is selected and click **OK.**

    d. Save the file as *My CSS Week12.mpp* and leave it open.

---

3. Check the current dates against the interim plan.

    a. Add **Start1** and **Finish1** columns to the view.

    b. Verify that the **Start1/Finish1** column dates correspond to the dates in the **Start/Finish** columns.

    c. Click the **Finish** cell for task 15 and change the date to **9/22/11.**

    d. Observe that the change is not reflected in the **Finish1** column.

TOPIC G
Create a Custom Table

In the previous topic, you set an interim plan in your project plan. You would also like to display interim dates along with baseline dates for tasks, in order to compare the two, but there is no default table in Project that shows this information. In this topic, you will create a custom table to display the information that you want.

As a project progresses, there is a great deal of information that can be viewed and analyzed to ascertain the condition of various aspects of the project. Such monitoring is vital to answer crucial questions such as—Are costs within budget? Is the project on schedule? Will deliverables be ready for hand off as planned? Unfortunately, switching between tables and views is often necessary to gauge the answers to such questions. Custom tables can be used to consolidate data, eliminating the confusion of switching between tables to view the desired information.

How to Create a Custom Table

Procedure Reference: Create a Custom Table

To create a custom table:

1. Choose **View→Tables→More Tables** to display the **More Tables** dialog box.
2. If necessary, select **Task** or **Resource** as appropriate.
3. Display the **Table Definition** dialog box.
   - Click **New** to create a new custom table or;
   - In the **Tables** list box, select the appropriate table and click **Copy** to create a copy of the selected table.
4. If necessary, specify table options in the **Table Definition** dialog box.
   - In the **Name** text box, type a suitable name.
   - Check the **Show in menu** check box to display the custom table on the **Table** submenu.
5. If necessary, in the **Field Name** column, select the appropriate column name and click **Delete Row** to delete the selected column from the table.
6. Add columns to the custom table as needed.
   - Add a column between the existing columns.
     a. If necessary, in the **Field Name** column, select the appropriate column and click **Insert Row.**
     b. In the **Field Name** column, from the **Field Name** drop-down list, select the desired column and press **Enter.**
   - Add a column as the last column.
     a. In the **Field Name** column, click below the last column name to display a drop-down arrow.
     b. From the **Field Name** drop-down list, select the appropriate column name and press **Enter.**
7. When you are done adding and deleting columns, click **OK.**

8. View the custom table.

   - In the **More Tables** dialog box, in the **Tables** list box, select the custom table and click **Apply** or;

   - Close the **More Tables** dialog box, then click the **View** tab, then choose **Tables→ More Tables** and select the custom table.

Custom Columns

You can also create custom columns to suit your needs, when none of the existing columns allow you to store data that you feel is relevant. Choose the **Format** tab, and choose **Insert Column** to access the **Insert Column** drop-down. From there, you can either type a new column name, or choose an existing column to add. This menu can also be accessed by right-clicking on a column header and choosing **Insert Column.**

ACTIVITY 2-7

Creating a Custom Table to Compare Interim and Baseline Dates

Before You Begin:

The My CSS Week 12.mpp file is open.

Scenario:

You have set an interim plan in the project plan for the CSS Training Manual project. You wish to compare these interim dates with the baseline dates. However, this information is not available in any of Project's existing tables. A colleague suggests creating a custom table based on the **Baseline** table to display only interim dates and baseline dates for tasks.

---

1.   Make a copy of the **Baseline** table.

    a.   From the **View** tab, display the **More Tables** dialog box.

    b.   In the **Tables** list box, select **Baseline** and click **Copy** to display the **Table Definition** dialog box.

---

2.   Define the custom table.

    a.   In the **Table Definition in 'CSS Week12.mpp'** dialog box, in the **Name** text box, type *BASELINE/INTERIM DATES*

    b.   In the **Field Name** column, select **Baseline Duration** and click **Delete Row**.

    c.   Delete the **Baseline Work** and **Baseline Cost** columns.

    d.   In the **Field Name** column, below the **Baseline Finish** field, from the **Field Name** drop-down list, select **Start1**.

    e.   Below the **Start1** field, from the **Field Name** drop-down list, select **Finish1**.

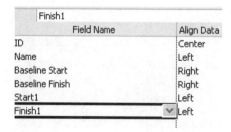

Finish1	
Field Name	Align Data
ID	Center
Name	Left
Baseline Start	Right
Baseline Finish	Right
Start1	Left
Finish1	Left

    f.   Click **OK** to add the **BASELINE/INTERIM DATES** table to the **Tables** list box in the **More Tables** dialog box.

---

3.   Display the **BASELINE/INTERIM DATES** table and add it to the **Table** submenu.

    a.   In the **Tables** list box, verify that **BASELINE/INTERIM DATES** is selected and click **Apply**.

---

b. Adjust the divide bar and widen the **Start1** and **Finish1** columns to view the data.

c. Observe that the **BASELINE/INTERIM DATES** table is displayed in the current view.

d. Display the **More Tables** dialog box.

e. In the **Tables** list box, verify that **BASELINE/INTERIM DATES** is selected and click **Edit.**

f. In the **Table Definition in 'My CSS Week12.mpp'** dialog box, check the **Show in menu** check box and click **OK.**

g. Close the **More Tables** dialog box.

h. In the **Data** group, click **Tables.**

i. Observe that the **BASELINE/INTERIM DATES** table is listed on the **Table** submenu and close the **Table** submenu.

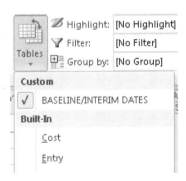

j. Save the file and close it.

TOPIC H
Create a Custom Field

In the previous topic, you created a custom table. There are times, however, when you do not need a custom entity as large as a table; a simple custom field in an existing table will suffice. In this topic, you will create a custom field.

Over the course of a project, the need to track and report on unanticipated information might arise. Project allows for all kinds of customization, allowing you to avoid being locked in to a particular view, table, report, or field. Custom fields are useful for those times when you want to display custom information, or perform a calculation on existing data and display the result. Being able to create custom fields helps keep Project as flexible as possible for your needs, as well as the needs of stakeholders and team members.

Custom Fields

Definition:

A *custom field* is a way to add additional attributes and functionality to tasks, resources, assignments, or projects. Custom fields can display text, a graphic, or the results of a calculation or formula.

Example:

Figure 2-8: Adding functionality using the Custom Fields dialog box.

The Custom Fields Dialog Box

After adding a custom field, you can choose to edit a number of features about that field by using the zones in the **Custom Fields** dialog box.

Zone	Description
Field	Allows you to specify if the custom field is for a task or resource, and allows you to choose a data type for the information to be added to that field. Data types include Cost, Date, Duration, Finish, Flag, Number, Start, Text, or Outline Code. This zone also allows you to rename, delete, or import a field, as well as add the custom field to the Enterprise using Project Server.
Custom attributes	Allows you to choose among **None, Lookup,** and **Formula. Lookup** and **Formula** each launch their own dialog boxes with additional options.
Calculation for task and group summary rows	Allows you to choose **None, Rollup,** or **Use Formula.**
Calculation for assignment rows	Allows you to choose either **None** or **Roll down** unless manually entered.
Values to display	Allows you to choose whether the display is to be a data value or a graphical indicator. Selecting **Graphical Indicators** launches a dialog box that allows you to choose additional options.

How to Create a Custom Field

Procedure Reference: Create a Custom Field

To create a custom field:

1. Using a method of your choice, create a new column in your project plan and assign a name to the new column.

2. Select the **Project** tab and click **Custom Fields** to display the **Custom Fields** dialog box.

3. In the **Field** zone, specify the options.

   - Choose whether the custom field will be for a Task or a Resource.

   - Specify the data type from the **Type** drop-down list.

   - Ensure that the proper field is selected in the **Field** area.

   - Choose **Rename, Delete, Add Field to Enterprise,** or **Import Field** as appropriate.

    It is not always possible to select **Add Field to Enterprise** because this syncs data about the custom field from the Project client to the Project Server.

4. In the **Custom attributes** zone, choose **None,** or click the **Lookup** or **Formula** button to launch their respective dialog boxes.

5. In the **Calculation for task and group summary rows** zone, ensure that **None** is selected. If the data type allows it, select **Rollup** or **Use formula.**

6. In the **Calculation for assignment rows** zone, choose either **None** or **Roll down unless manually entered.**

7. In the **Values to display** zone, choose either **Data** or **Graphical Indicators.**
8. Click **OK.**

ACTIVITY 2-8
Creating a Custom Field

Data Files:

C:\084603Data\Updating a Project Plan\CSS Week13.mpp

Scenario:

In an effort to better estimate the workload for similar projects, your manager has asked all the project managers to provide information on which of their tasks have gone over baseline and which have stayed under. To make it easier to see which tasks are affected, and to avoid hunting for relevant information within the table, you decide to add a custom column and icons to quickly represent the information that your manager wants to see.

---

1. Open and view the **Work** table.

    a. From the C:\084603Data\Updating a Project Plan folder, open the CSS Week13.mpp file.

    b. If necessary, on the **View** tab, choose **Tables→Work.**

    c. If necessary, drag the vertical bar to expose more of the **Work** table.

---

2. Add a custom field to the **Work** table.

    a. Click in the **Add New Column** column and enter *Workload Summary*

    b. On the **Project** tab, choose **Custom Fields.**

    c. In the **Custom Fields** dialog box, verify that **Task** is selected, and that the **Type** drop-down reads **Text.**

    d. In the **Custom attributes** zone, select the **Lookup** option button and then click the **Lookup** button.

    e. In the **Lookup table** zone, in the **Value** column, in the first cell, type *Above*

    f. In the **Lookup table** zone, in the **Value** column, in the second cell, type *Below* and press **Enter.**

g.   Check the **Use a value from the table as the default entry for the field** check box and then click **Close.**

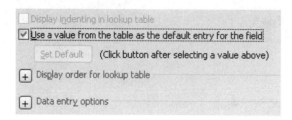

3.   Add graphical indicators to the custom fields.

a.   In the **Custom Fields** dialog box, in the **Values to display** zone, select the **Graphical Indicators** option button and then click the **Graphical Indicators** button.

b.   In the first row of the **Test for 'Workload Summary'** column, click the drop-down arrow and choose **equals.**

c.   In the first row of the **Value(s)** column, click in the field and type *Above*

d.   In the first row of the **Image** column, click in the field, click the drop-down arrow, and scroll down to select the green smiling face icon.

e.   In the second row of the **Test for 'Workload Summary'** column, click the drop-down arrow and choose **equals.**

f.   In the second row of the **Value(s)** column, click in the field and type *Below*

g.   In the second row of the **Image** column, click in the field, click the drop-down arrow, and scroll down to select the red frowning face icon.

h.   Click **OK** to close the **Graphical Indicators** dialog box and then click **OK** to close the **Custom Fields** dialog box.

4.   Add information to selected fields in the new column.

a.   In the **Workload Summary** column, click in the cell for task 3, click the drop-down arrow, and select **Above.**

b.   Note that the word **Above** is not displayed and that the green smiling face icon is displayed instead. Click in the **Workload Summary** cell for task 5.

c.   Click the drop-down arrow and select **Below.**

d.   Note that the red smiling face icon appears.

e.   Save the file as *My CSS Week13.mpp* and click **Close.**

Lesson 2 Follow-up

In this lesson, you updated your project plan with task progress information as work on the project progressed. This helps you steer the project to completion on time and within the stipulated budget as you are better prepared to handle any potential problem.

1. **What are the potential consequences if a plan is not updated regularly throughout the course of a project?**

2. **What factors will prompt you to create custom tables and fields? What are the advantages of custom tables and fields?**

3 Managing Project Costs

Lesson Time: 1 hour(s)

Lesson Objectives:

In this lesson, you will manage project costs.

You will:

- Update cost rate tables in a project plan.
- Group costs by budget type.
- Link a document to a project plan.

Introduction

In the previous lesson, you updated a project plan with task progress information. However, keeping your project plan up to date and on track also involves dealing with financial information. In this lesson, you will manage project costs.

Managing a project's costs is an important aspect of controlling the project. Many circumstances can necessitate updating the cost rates of resources—employees' salaries could increase, prices of materials could rise or fall over time, different grades of materials charging different rates could be utilized in the project, and so on. Such updates affect the project's costs. Therefore, monitoring the project's costs with the aid of any relevant information is a good practice to successfully manage project costs.

TOPIC A
Update Cost Rate Tables

Project has features that help you manage a project's costs. When multiple rates are to be charged by resources working on tasks, or future rates need to be specified, the project plan should be updated accordingly. In this topic, you will update cost rate tables.

Conditions vary during the course of a project. Employees' salaries could increase during the course of a project. Costs of materials could rise or fall. Different grades of materials that charge different rates could be used on tasks. Different rates could be charged by the same resource on different tasks. In such cases, the project plan should be updated so that the appropriate rates are charged for work done on tasks.

Cost Rate Tables

Cost rate tables for a particular resource can be seen on the **Costs** tab of the **Resource Information** dialog box. They store a resource's rates and the date from which these rates come into effect. Project provides cost rate tables for work and material resources, but not for cost resources. There are five cost rate tables available per resource—**A, B, C, D,** and **E.** These tables cannot be renamed and **A** is the default table. The separate cost rate tables allow a resource to charge different rates for separate tasks. Each table contains 25 rows. The separate rows can be used to specify future increases and decreases in rates for a given task.

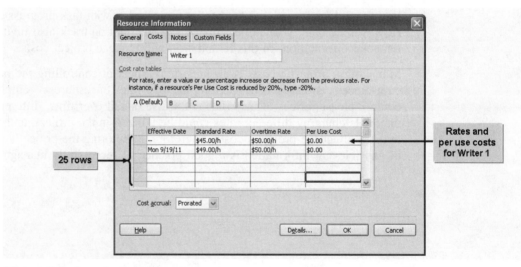

Figure 3-1: A cost rate table.

 The first row of every cost rate table holds the default rate, if a rate is specified. No effective date is associated with the default rate. So, the **Effective Date** column contains two dashes. You cannot set an effective date in this row.

Calculation of Task Cost

When a resource is assigned to work on a task, the resource's rates in the assigned cost rate table are used by Project to calculate the cost of work done on that task. Per use cost for the resource and fixed cost for the task also add to the cost of a task. The **Cost** column shows the cost for the whole task regardless of how much work has actually been completed. The **Actual** column shows the cost incurred so far based on the amount of work completed and the cost accrual method. The **Remaining** column shows the difference between the values in the **Actual** and **Cost** columns. These columns can be seen in the **Cost** table.

How to Update Cost Rate Tables

Procedure Reference: Update a Cost Rate Table

To update a cost rate table:

1. Display the **Resource Sheet** view.

2. In the **Resource Information** dialog box for the appropriate resource, select the **Costs** tab.

3. On the **Costs** page, update the cost rate tables.

   - Specify multiple rates for a resource.

     a. Select the appropriate tab to display the desired cost rate table.

     b. In the first row of the selected cost rate table, in the **Standard Rate** column, enter an appropriate value to set the standard hourly rate.

     c. If necessary, in the **Overtime Rate** and **Per Use Cost** columns, enter appropriate values.

     d. If necessary, specify additional rates in other cost rate tables.

   - Specify future rates that will come into effect after a specified date.

     a. If necessary, select the appropriate tab to display the desired cost rate table.

     b. In the first blank row of the selected cost rate table, from the **Effective Date** calendar, select an appropriate date.

     c. In the same row, in the **Standard Rate** column, type a numeric value, or type a percentage increase or decrease as appropriate and press **Enter.**

     d. If necessary, in the **Overtime Rate** and **Per Use Cost** columns, enter appropriate values.

4. Click **OK.**

Procedure Reference: Set a Different Cost Rate Table for an Assignment

To set a different cost rate table for an assignment:

1. Display the **Task Usage** or **Resource Usage** view.

2. Set a different cost rate table for a particular assignment.

   - Set a different cost rate table in the **Cost Rate Table** column.

     a. Insert the **Cost Rate Table** column.

     b. If necessary, reposition the **Cost Rate Table** column.

     c. In the **Cost Rate Table** column, from the **Cost Rate Table** drop-down list corresponding to the appropriate assignment, select the desired cost rate table.

An assignment is a resource working on a particular task.

d. Press **Enter.**

• Set a different cost rate table in the **Assignment Information** dialog box.

a. Double-click the appropriate resource or task corresponding to the desired assignment to display the **Assignment Information** dialog box.

b. On the **General** page, from the **Cost rate table** drop-down list, select the appropriate cost rate table.

c. Click **OK.**

ACTIVITY 3-1

Updating Cost Rate Tables in a Project Plan

Data Files:

C:\084603Data\Managing Project Costs\HTML Week1.mpp

Scenario:

The HTML Training Manual project is proceeding as planned. However, in the status meeting today, you were notified of some resource cost changes that will affect your project plan. Writer 1 has received a salary raise of 15%, which will be effective on Thursday, Sep. 1, 2011, and the paper used for the Print Final task is a more expensive grade of paper that costs $9.50 per ream. You need to update the project plan to reflect these changes.

---

1. Display the **Resource Information** dialog box for Writer 1.

   a. Open the C:\084603Data\Managing Project Costs\HTML Week1.mpp file.

   b. Switch to the **Resource Sheet** view.

   c. Double-click "Writer 1" to display the **Resource Information** dialog box.

---

2. Enter a salary raise of 15% for Writer 1, coming into effect on 9/1/11.

   a. Display the **Costs** tab of the **Resource Information** dialog box.

   b. On the **A (Default)** page, in the second row of the cost rate table, set the **Effective Date** as **9/1/11.**

   c. In the **Standard Rate** column, enter **+15%** so that a future salary raise is available for Writer 1.

   d. In the **Overtime Rate** column, enter **+15%** so that a future salary raise is available for Writer 1.

   e. Observe that the cost rate table gets updated and click **OK.**

f.   Display the **Cost** table and observe that the costs highlighted in the **Cost** table for Writer 1 have increased.

Writer 1	$18,486.00	$17,280.00	$1,206.00	$5,040.00	$13,446.00
Editor 1	$952.00	$952.00	$0.00	$0.00	$952.00
Printer 1	$160.00	$160.00	$0.00	$0.00	$160.00
Artist 1	$1,000.00	$1,000.00	$0.00	$0.00	$1,000.00
Project Manager 1	$480.00	$480.00	$0.00	$480.00	$0.00
Staff Assistant 1	$192.00	$192.00	$0.00	$192.00	$0.00
Account Rep 1	$0.00	$0.00	$0.00	$0.00	$0.00
Publisher 1	$384.62	$384.62	$0.00	$384.62	$0.00
Subject Matter Expert	$4,000.00	$4,800.00	($800.00)	$2,400.00	$1,600.00
Paper	$15.00	$15.00	$0.00	$0.00	$15.00
Airfare	$250.00	$250.00	$0.00	$0.00	$250.00
Lodging	$200.00	$200.00	$0.00	$0.00	$200.00

3.   Create an alternative rate of $9.50 in the cost rate table **B** for the resource "Paper."

a.   Double-click "Paper" to display the **Resource Information** dialog box.

b.   On the **Costs** tab, click **B** to display the cost rate table **B**.

c.   In the **Standard Rate** column, enter a value of *$9.50*

d.   Click **OK.**

4.   Assign cost rate table **B** to task 23 in the **Cost** table of the **Task Usage** view.

a.   Switch to the **Task Usage** view.

b.   On the **View** tab, in the **Data** section, from the **Tables** drop-down list, select the **Cost** table.

c.   Drag the divide bar to display all the columns of the **Cost** table.

d.   Insert the **Cost Rate Table** column as a new column.

e.   For the resource "Paper" assigned to task 23, from the **Cost Rate Table** drop-down list, select **B** and press **Enter.**

f.   Observe how the values for task 23 and its summary task increase as a result.

⊟ Print final	$89.50	$87.50	$2.00	$0.00	$89.50	
Printer 1	$80.00	$80.00	$0.00	$0.00	$80.00	A
Paper	$9.50	$7.50	$2.00	$0.00	$9.50	B

g.   Save the file as *My HTML Week1.mpp* and close it.

TOPIC B
Group Costs

In the previous topic, you updated cost rate tables in the project plan. In addition to keeping track of cost rates, you will also need to display costs arranged according to criteria of your specification. In this topic, you will group costs.

As your project progresses, you may be called upon to periodically report on its finances. To do this effectively, you need to be aware of the project costs. Grouping costs by relevant criteria helps you gain better insight into a project's costs. It also helps you determine whether costs are within set limits, as well as identify the tasks or resources that have resulted in higher or lower costs than expected, and so on.

Groups

Definition:

Groups are a method of organizing information presented in a view, according to specific criteria. Applying a group to a view displays information in categories with summarized information for each category. The groups available differ depending on the type of the current view such as task groups for task views and resource groups for resource views. The **More Groups** dialog box provides options to create new groups and edit existing groups.

Example:

Figure 3-2: Groups in the More Groups dialog box.

The Group Column

The **Group** column in the **Resource Sheet** view corresponds to the **Resource Group** option in the **Group by** drop-down. Selecting this option organizes a view based on the values in the **Group** column.

The Group Definition Dialog Box

The **Group Definition** dialog box allows the creation of new groups when none of the existing groups meet your needs. This dialog box provides options to group information based on custom columns as well as the predefined ones. It enables grouping by multiple criteria. You can specify ordering within the group other than the default ascending order. You can also group assignments and specify formatting for data that matches a particular grouping criterion. Once created, a new group can be added to the **Group by** drop-down.

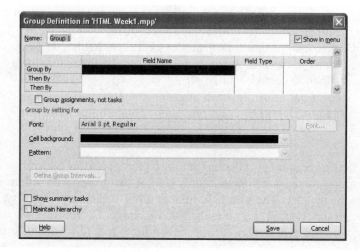

Figure 3-3: Options in the Group Definition dialog box.

How to Group Costs

Procedure Reference: Group Costs Using the Group Definition Dialog Box

To group costs using the **Group Definition** dialog box:

1. Display the **Cost** table, or insert the appropriate columns in the desired view.
2. On the **View** tab, in the **Data** section, choose **Group by→More Groups** to display the **More Groups** dialog box.
3. If necessary, select **Task** or **Resource** to specify the type of group to create.
4. Click **New** to display the **Group Definition** dialog box.
5. In the **Group Definition** dialog box, specify the desired settings.
    *   In the **Name** text box, type a suitable name for the new group.
    *   Check the **Show in menu** check box to display the new group on the **Group by** submenu.
    *   Check the **Group assignments, not tasks** or **Group assignments, not resources** check box to display only resources or tasks, respectively.
    *   In the **Group Definition** table, specify the grouping criteria.
        a. In the **Field Name** column, from the **Field Name** drop-down list corresponding to **Group By,** select the desired column name.
        b. If necessary, in the **Order** column, select **Ascending** or **Descending** to sort results in ascending or descending order, respectively.

    c.   If necessary, in the remaining **Then By** rows of the **Group Definition** table, specify more grouping criteria.

- In the **Group by setting for** section, select the required **Group By** or **Then By** row and specify the desired font, cell background color, and pattern to be applied to tasks or resources that match the grouping criteria.

6.   If necessary, define group intervals for the selected grouping criterion.

    a.   Click **Define Group Intervals** to display the **Define Group Interval** dialog box.

    b.   From the **Group on** drop-down list and in the **Start at** and **Group interval** spin boxes, select the appropriate values.

7.   Click **OK** to display the new group in the **More Groups** dialog box.

8.   Click **Apply** to apply the new group to the current view.

Procedure Reference: Create a Custom Group

To create a custom group:

1.   Display the **Cost** table, or insert the appropriate columns in the desired view.

2.   On the **View** tab, in the **Data** section, choose **Group by→New Group By.**

3.   In the **Group Definition** dialog box, specify the desired settings for the custom group.

4.   In the **Customize Group By** dialog box, click **Apply** to apply the custom group to the current view, or click **Save** to save the group in the **Group By** list.

ACTIVITY 3-2
Grouping Costs by Budget Type

Data Files:

C:\084603Data\Managing Project Costs\HTML Week2.mpp

Scenario:

Now that the HTML Training Manual project has started, the project stakeholders may ask for an update on how the costs incurred so far compare to the allowances set forth in the budget. To prepare for the upcoming meeting, you need to create a budget type group in Project, so you can further analyze the costs.

---

1. Insert the **Actual Work** and **Actual Cost** columns in the **Resource Usage** view.

    a. From the C:\084603Data\Managing Project Costs folder, open the HTML Week2.mpp file.

    b. Switch to the **Resource Usage** view.

    c. To the right of the **Work** column, insert the **Actual Work** column.

    d. To the right of the **Actual Work** column, insert the **Actual Cost** column.

    e. Arrange the columns in the order **Resource Name, Budget Work, Actual Work, Work, Budget Cost, Actual Cost,** and **Cost.**

---

2. Create a new group with the grouping criterion, budget type.

    a. On the **View** tab, in the **Data** section, choose **Group by→More Groups** to display the **More Groups** dialog box.

    b. Click **New** to display the **Group Definition in 'HTML Week2.mpp'** dialog box.

    c. In the **Name** text box, type *Budget Type Group*

    d. In the first row of the **Group Definition** table, from the **Field Name** drop-down list, select **Budget Type (Text1).**

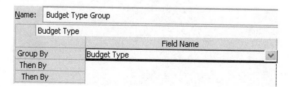

    e. Click **Save** to add the new group to the **More Groups** dialog box.

---

3. Apply the new group to the current view.

    a. Click **Apply** to apply the new group to the **Resource Usage** view.

    b. Widen the **Resource Name** column so that the data in this column is visible.

---

c. Observe that the first category is the **Budget Type: Labor Budget** category.

d. Scroll down to display the **Budget Type: Material Budget** and **Budget Type: Travel & Stay Budget** categories.

e. Scroll back to the top and collapse the **Budget Type: Labor Budget** category so that only its summary information is displayed.

⊞ Budget Type: Labor Budget	576 hrs	168 hrs		$9,252.62	$26,626.62
⊟ Budget Type: Material Budget				$0.00	$17.00
⊟ Paper		0 reams		$0.00	$17.00
Print proof		0 reams		$0.00	$7.50
Print final		0 reams		$0.00	$9.50
⊟ Budget - Material	3 reams				
HTML Training Manual	3 reams				
⊟ Budget Type: Travel & Stay Budget			$1,000.00	$0.00	$450.00
⊟ Airfare				$0.00	$250.00
Present to publisher				$0.00	$250.00
⊟ Lodging				$0.00	$200.00
Present to publisher				$0.00	$200.00
⊟ Budget - Travel&Stay			$1,000.00		
HTML Training Manual			$1,000.00		

f. Save the file as ***My HTML Week2.mpp*** and close it.

ACTIVITY 3-3
Grouping Costs by Multiple Criteria

Data Files:

C:\084603Data\Managing Project Costs\HTML Week3.mpp

Scenario:

To prepare for the upcoming status meeting for the HTML Training Manual project, you must be familiar with the monthly expenditures and how the critical and noncritical tasks are affected. To analyze this specific information, you will create a group to display the required information in a customized format.

1.   Display the **Cost** table in the **Task Usage** view.

    a.   From the C:\084603Data\Managing Project Costs folder, open the HTML Week3.mpp file.

    b.   Switch to the **Task Usage** view.

    c.   Display the **Cost** table.

    d.   Drag the divide bar to display all the columns of the **Cost** table.

2.   Create a custom group to group costs by critical and noncritical tasks in a monthly break-down.

    a.   On the **View** tab, in the **Data** section, choose **Group by→New Group By.**

    b.   In the **Name** text box, type *My Custom Costs Group*

    c.   In the **Group By** row of the **Group Definition** table, from the **Field Name** drop-down list, select **Critical.**

    d.   In the **Then By** row of the **Group Definition** table, from the **Field Name** drop-down list, select **Start.**

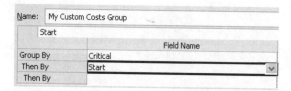

    e.   Click **Define Group Intervals** to launch the **Define Group Interval** dialog box.

    f.   From the **Group on** drop-down list, select **Months.**

g. Observe that the **Start at** text box contains the project's start date and the **Group Interval** is set to **1** and then click **OK.**

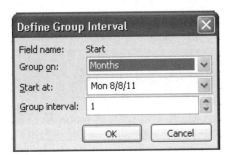

h. Click **Save** to save the custom group to the **Group By** menu.

3. Check whether the group information is displayed.

   a. From the **Group by** drop-down list, in the **Custom** section, click **My Custom Costs Group.**

   b. If necessary, widen the **Task Name** column.

   c. If necessary, scroll down to see the categories that are newly created.

   d. Collapse the monthly categories under **Critical: No** and **Critical: Yes.**

   e. Save the file as *My HTML Week3.mpp* and close it.

TOPIC C
Link Documents to a Project Plan

In the previous topic, you grouped costs by relevant criteria. For ease of understanding, you wish to provide a document detailing budget types for reference. In this topic, you will link a document to the project plan.

During the course of a project, situations may arise where you wish to incorporate additional information into a project plan. This supplemental information could provide clarity on the details of the project plan with respect to company guidelines. However, as project plans generally contain a lot of information, keeping file size to a minimum is desirable. You can meet both these needs by linking external documents to your project plan.

Hyperlinks

Definition:

In Project, a *hyperlink* is an interactive icon, which, when clicked, links to a location in the current project plan, a file in its corresponding application, a web page in a browser, or a new Message form in Outlook for an email address. Hyperlinks are displayed in the **Indicators** column. Only one hyperlink can be attached to any task, resource, or assignment. A default screentip is assigned to a hyperlink. However, a screentip of your choice can be specified. Hyperlinks keep the project plan's file size to a minimum because they store only the location of the object they link to, rather than the entire object.

Example:

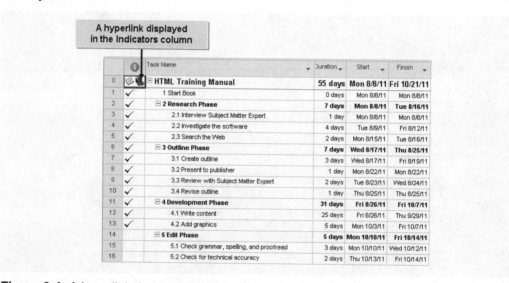

Figure 3-4: A hyperlink that is displayed in the Indicators column.

Adding Supporting Information to a Project Plan

There are several methods of adding supporting information to a project plan.

Method	Description
Add a note to a task, resource, or assignment	Notes are for adding information such as reminders, hyperlinks, or links to offsite files.
Create hyperlink to supporting information	Hyperlinks are links to files that are stored elsewhere; you may add a direct link to another file, but the file size of the project plan is not increased because the linked file is not actually part of the project plan.
Copy and paste supporting information	As with other Office applications, copying and pasting makes text part of the current file, thus increasing the file size. This is most useful for small bits of text, small graphics, and so on.
Embed supporting information	Information can be embedded in a project plan as an object. This increases the overall file size of the plan. You edit the object in its associated source program, but not directly in the project plan. When the object is edited in its source program, the changes are not automatically reflected in the project plan.
Link to supporting information	Unlike an embedded object, a linked object does not increase the file size of the project plan, and any change made in the source program is reflected immediately in the project plan.
Use SharePoint to manage supporting information	If you use Project Server in conjunction with Windows SharePoint Server, project-related documents can be managed centrally.

Embed a File in a Project Plan

To embed a file in a project plan, select the **Notes** tab of the **Task Information** or **Resource Information** dialog box and click **Insert Object.** The **Insert Object** dialog box allows you to create a new file to embed, or to embed a copy of an existing file. In the latter case, you can choose to maintain a link between the embedded file and the original file by checking the **Link** check box. When a link is maintained, any change saved in the embedded file is updated in the source file and vice versa. The embedded file can be represented by an icon corresponding to the appropriate file type if the **Display As Icon** check box is checked. Remember that when a file is embedded in the plan, the overall plan file size increases.

In Project 2010, the **Insert Object** dialog box needs to be manually added to the Ribbon. To do this, on the **File** tab, choose **Options→Customize Ribbon.** From the **Choose commands from** drop-down list, select **All commands** and then select **Object.** Before clicking **Add,** you will first need to create a custom group for the **Insert Object** dialog box to be stored in.

How to Link Documents to a Project Plan

Procedure Reference: Link a Document to a Project Plan by Using Hyperlinks

To link a document to a project plan by using hyperlinks:

1. Select the task, resource, or assignment to which a document is to be linked.

2. Right-click the task, resource, or assignment and choose **Hyperlink** to display the **Insert Hyperlink** dialog box.

3. Specify an item to link to.

   ● Link to an existing file or a web page.

      a. Select **Existing File or Web Page.**

      b. In the **Look in** section, browse for the desired file or web page.

      c. Select the desired file or web page so that the path to it is displayed in the **Address** text box.

   ● Link to a location within the project plan.

      a. Select **Place in This Document.**

      b. In the **Select a view in this project** list box, select the appropriate view.

      c. In the **Enter the task or resource ID** text box, type a numeric value indicating the task or resource to link to.

   ● Link to a newly created document.

      a. Select **Create New Document.**

      b. In the **Name of new document** text box, type a suitable file name with the appropriate file extension.

      c. Click the **Change** button to browse to a different location in which the document will be created.

      d. Select **Edit the new document later** or **Edit the new document now** as appropriate.

   ● Link to an email address.

      a. Select **E-mail Address.**

      b. In the **E-mail address** text box, enter the desired address.

      c. In the **Subject** text box, enter a subject.

      d. Click **OK** to insert a link to an email address.

4. If desired, click on the **ScreenTip** button, type the desired text, and click **OK** to set a screentip for the new hyperlink.

5. Click **OK** so that a hyperlink is displayed in the **Indicators** column for the particular task, resource, or assignment.

6. Click the hyperlink to test it.

Edit a Hyperlink

An existing hyperlink can be edited through the **Edit Hyperlink** dialog box. This dialog box can be accessed by right-clicking the hyperlink and choosing **Hyperlink→Edit Hyperlink.**

Procedure Reference: Remove a Hyperlink

To remove a hyperlink:

1. Select the task, resource, or assignment to which the hyperlink corresponds.

2. Move the mouse pointer over the hyperlink in the **Indicators** column.

3. Right-click and choose **Hyperlink**→**Clear Hyperlinks** to remove the hyperlink from the **Indicators** column.

ACTIVITY 3-4
Linking a Document to a Project Plan

Data Files:

C:\084603Data\Managing Project Costs\HTML Week4.mpp, C:\084603Data\Managing Project Costs\BudgetTypes.docx

Scenario:

Now that your project plan is updated with specific groups that provide information on costs, your manager has also requested that the company's approved budget types be available for reference within the project plan. You will create a hyperlink from the project summary task to the Budget Types document.

---

1. Link the Word document to the project's summary task.

    a. From the C:\084603Data\Managing Project Costs folder, open the HTML Week4.mpp file.

    b. Right-click on the **HTML Training Manual** project summary task and choose **Hyperlink** to display the **Insert Hyperlink** dialog box.

    c. If necessary, select **Existing File or Web Page.**

    d. In the **Look in** section, navigate to the C:\084603Data\Managing Project Costs folder and select the **BudgetTypes.docx** file.

    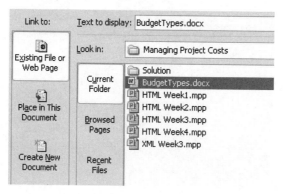

    e. In the **Insert Hyperlink** dialog box, click **OK.**

    f. Place the mouse pointer over the hyperlink in the **Indicators** column to display a screentip that indicates the document it links to.

---

2. Append the text "Guidelines on Budget Types" to the hyperlink's screentip.

a. Right-click the hyperlink and choose **Hyperlink→Edit Hyperlink** to display the **Edit Hyperlink** dialog box.

b. Click **ScreenTip** to display the **Set Hyperlink ScreenTip** dialog box.

c. In the **ScreenTip text** text box, type *Guidelines on Budget Types* and click **OK.**

d. Click **OK** to close the **Edit Hyperlink** dialog box.

e. Place the mouse pointer over the hyperlink to display the edited screentip.

3. Test the hyperlink.

a. In the **Indicators** column, right-click the hyperlink and choose **Hyperlink→Open Hyperlink** to open the Word document.

b. In the **Microsoft Office Project Security Notice** message box, click **Yes.**

c. Close the Word document.

d. Maximize the Project application.

e. Save the file as *My HTML Week4.mpp* and close it.

Lesson 3 Follow-up

In this lesson, you covered the skills necessary to manage project costs. This knowledge helps you ensure that your project plan contains accurate, up-to-date financial information and you are in a better position to handle any problem that may crop up.

1. **When will you want to update cost rate tables in your projects?**

2. **What do you think are the advantages of grouping costs by relevant criteria?**

4 Reporting Project Data Visually

Lesson Time: 1 hour(s)

Lesson Objectives:

In this lesson, you will report project data visually.

You will:

● Create a visual report.

● Customize a visual report.

● Create a visual report template.

Introduction

In the previous lesson, you updated the cost information in your project plan. When presenting project data such as project cost to stakeholders, it might be beneficial to use visually appealing reports, to enable better comprehension. In this lesson, you will create and use visual reports to represent project information.

Sometimes, you may have to present your project report either to managers or to project stakeholders. If the report contains too much information, or if it contains too many columns in the view you have printed, it might be difficult for your audience to properly understand the meaning of the information. To help your audience understand better, you might consider preparing a visual report that summarizes and clarifies the raw, numerical data.

TOPIC A
Create a Visual Report

In the previous lessons, you used the various views in Project to examine a project's status, track its progress, identify problems, and more. Though you can print the different views to report this data, the specific data that you need might be spread across a number of views, and is therefore impossible to print from one single view. In this topic, you will create a visual report with customized, relevant project information.

While it might be possible to include a lot of information about a project when it comes time to report on it, you run the risk of overwhelming your audience with confusing, irrelevant data. To help prevent information overload, you can prepare reports that use only the relevant numbers that you specify, regardless of which view they appear in by default, and you can present them in a visually appealing way. This helps ensure that your audience is better able to understand how the numbers impact them, and it ensures that you can share only relevant data with different project stakeholders.

Visual Reports

Definition:

Visual reports are graphical representations of project data in the form of charts. These visual reports are created as charts and tables in Excel or Visio. Project provides users with a variety of built-in visual report templates that can be used to create reports.

Example:

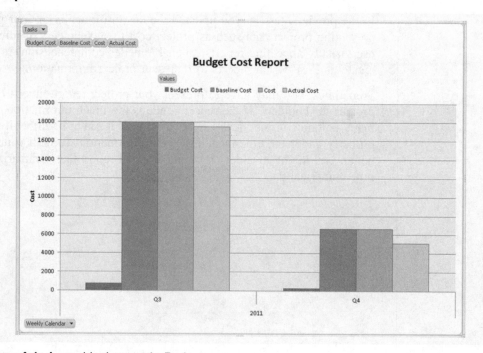

Figure 4-1: *A graphical report in Project.*

The Visual Reports — Create Report Dialog Box

The **Visual Reports - Create Report** dialog box enables users to choose the type of visual report required from the built-in list of templates, and also edit its contents.

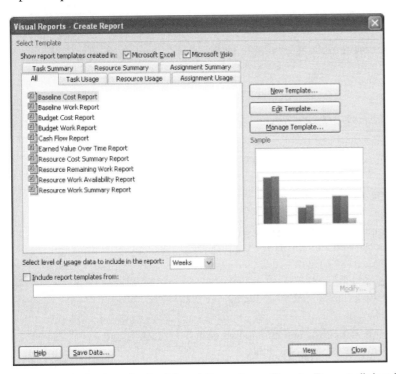

Figure 4-2: Options in the Visual Reports — Create Report dialog box.

Option	Description
Show report templates created in	Displays a list of predefined visual report templates that can be opened either in Excel or in Visio.
New Template	Displays the **Visual Reports - New Template** dialog box with options to select the type of application in which the report is to be created, data, and the fields that are to be inserted in the report.
Edit Template	Displays the **Visual Reports - Field Picker** dialog box. This dialog box allows the user to modify the fields that are used as base data in the report.
Manage Template	Displays the folder where the built-in templates are stored. By default, the custom templates are not stored along with the built-in templates, and can only be managed by using the **Manage Template** option.
Save Data	Displays the **Visual Reports - Save Reporting Data** dialog box, with options to export project data as OLAP cubes.

 On Line Analytical Processing, or OLAP, is a method of providing answers quickly to analytical queries that are multidimensional in nature. An OLAP cube is a specifically designed database that is similar to the two-dimensional array of a spreadsheet. OLAP cubes are used for optimizing a report and data retrieval.

Predefined Visual Report Templates

The **Visual Reports - Create Report** dialog box displays a list of built-in visual report templates that can be used for creating a report in Excel or Visio. You can view all of the available reports, or you can view them by category.

Visual Report Templates

There are a number of visual report templates available in Excel.

Visual Report Template	Type of Report Created	Category
Baseline Cost Report	A bar graph with the baseline cost, planned cost, and actual cost for the project across time.	Assignment Usage
Baseline Work Report	A bar graph with baseline work, planned work, and actual work for the project across time.	Assignment Usage
Budget Cost Report	A bar graph with budget cost, baseline cost, planned cost, and actual cost for the project over time.	Assignment Usage
Budget Work Report	A bar graph with budget work, baseline work, planned work, and actual work for the project over time.	Assignment Usage
Cash Flow Report	A bar graph with costs and cumulative cost amounts for the project over time.	Task Usage
Earned Value Over Time Report	A chart with actual cost of work performed, planned value, and earned value for the project over time.	Assignment Usage
Resource Cost Summary Report	A pie chart that illustrates the division of the resource cost among the different resource types.	Resource Usage
Resource Remaining Work Report	A bar graph with total resource capacity, work, remaining availability, and actual work.	Resource Summary
Resource Work Availability Report	A bar graph with total capacity, work, and remaining availability for work, and resources of a project over time.	Resource Usage
Resource Work Summary Report	A bar graph with total resource capacity, work, remaining availability, and actual work for a project.	Resource Usage

How to Create a Visual Report

Procedure Reference: Create a Visual Report by Using Predefined Templates

To create a visual report by using predefined templates:

1. Open the project plan for which a report is to be generated.

2. On the **Project** tab, select **Visual Reports.**

3. In the **Visual Reports - Create Report** dialog box, if necessary, select the **All** tab to view the list of all the available visual report templates.

 If you know the category to which the desired template belongs to, you can select the appropriate category's tab in the **Visual Reports - Create Report** dialog box to display a shorter list of templates.

4. In the **All** list box, select the desired visual report template based on which the report is to be generated.

5. If necessary, from the **Select level of usage data to include in the report** drop-down list, select the desired level of data to specify the duration of project data you wish to use in the report.

6. Click **View** to generate the report and open it.

ACTIVITY 4-1
Creating Visual Reports

Data Files:

C:\084603Data\Reporting Project Data Visually\CSS Report.mpp

Scenario:

Your colleague from accounting, Samantha Smith, is to present her quarterly report on each project's cost value over time. She has requested that you provide her with the cost flow details for the CSS Report project. Because she is not very familiar with Project, she has asked that you give her the details in an Excel file with graphics to help display the details clearly.

1. Display the **Assignment Usage** tab.

   a. From the C:\084603Data\Reporting Project Data Visually folder, open the CSS Report.mpp file.

   b. On the **Project** tab, click **Visual Reports.**

   c. In the **Visual Reports - Create Report** dialog box, select the **Assignment Usage** tab.

2. Generate the **Budget Cost Report.**

   a. On the **Assignment Usage** tab, select **Budget Cost Report.**

   b. The report preview appears in the **Sample** section. From the **Select level of usage data to include in the report** drop-down list, select **Quarters** to generate a report for the quarterly data.

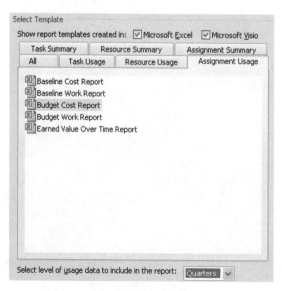

   c. Click **View** to generate the report.

3. View the report in Excel.

    a. In the adr11 [Compatibility Mode] - Microsoft Excel window, observe that the chart displays the project plan data.

    b. Open the **Assignment Usage** worksheet.

    c. Observe the cost data.

    d. Save the file as *My CSS Report.xlsx* in the C:\084603Data\Reporting Project Data Visually folder.

    e. Close the Excel workbook and the **Visual Reports - Create Report** dialog box.

TOPIC B
Customize a Visual Report

In the previous topic, you created a visual report using the project data. Now, you may want to modify certain features of the report to suit your current needs. In this topic, you will customize a visual report in Excel.

When preparing for a presentation, you may need to have a specific set of data that you are required to show the audience. However, the report created using Project's default options may not cater to your specific needs. Knowing how to create custom visual reports is an important step toward both managing a project effectively and ensuring that project stakeholders are kept up to date with relevant information.

PivotViews

In Project, when a visual report is generated, it is displayed as a **PivotChart** and **PivotTable.** The **PivotTable** contains data from the project plan. A **PivotChart** report is an interactive chart that graphically represents the data in a **PivotTable** report. **PivotChart** reports can be created only from an existing **PivotTable** report. Once a report is created, you can make changes to it by filtering the content or changing the layout.

PivotDiagrams in Visio

When a visual report is displayed in Visio, it is displayed as a **PivotDiagram.** This is similar to the **PivotTables** and **PivotCharts** displayed in Excel. The **PivotDiagrams** in Visio are mainly used for hierarchical data such as work breakdown structures. You can also customize these diagrams and perform calculations in them.

The PivotTable Field List Pane

The **PivotTable Field List** pane enables you to specify the source data that is to be used in the **PivotTable** and in the corresponding **PivotChart.**

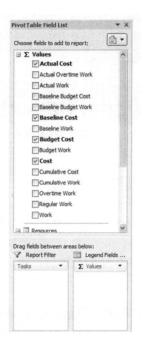

Figure 4-3: *The PivotTable Field List pane with options to specify source data.*

Section	Description
Choose fields to add to report	A section that is displayed at the top of the pane; it can be used for including and removing fields. The layout of the **PivotTable Field List** pane can be customized to suit individual requirements.
View	A drop-down menu that can be used to change the layout of the **PivotTable Field List** pane.
Drag fields between areas below	A section that is displayed at the bottom of the pane; it can be used for repositioning and rearranging the fields. This section has areas that allow you to drag fields into each of them.
	● The fields that are dragged into the **Report Filter** list box are used to filter the report based on the item selected in the report filter.
	● The fields that are dragged into the **Column Labels** list box are displayed as columns in the report. If there are two fields in the area, the second field is automatically nested below the first one.
	● The fields that are dragged into the **Row Labels** list box are displayed as columns in the report. If there are two fields in the area, the second field is automatically nested below the first one.
	● The fields that are dragged into the **Values** list box are used to display the summary of numeric data.
Defer layout update	A check box that can be checked to disable the updating of the **PivotTable** report when the fields are dragged into the areas. After having changed the layout of the report, you can click the **Update** button to view the changes in the report.

The **Axis Fields** and **Legend Fields** list boxes in the **Drag fields between areas below** section of the **PivotChart** correspond to the **Row Labels** and **Column Labels** list boxes in the **Drag fields between areas below** section of the **PivotTable**, respectively.

How to Customize a Visual Report

Procedure Reference: Format a Visual Report in Excel

To format a visual report in Excel:

1. Open the project plan whose report is to be generated.
2. On the **Project** tab, select **Visual Reports.**
3. In the **Visual Reports - Create Report** dialog box, select the desired settings and click **View.**
4. In the Excel workbook, use the contextual tabs to format the charts.
5. Save and close the report.

Procedure Reference: Customize a Visual Report by Using the Field Picker

To customize a visual report by using the field picker:

1. Display the **Visual Report - Create Report** dialog box.
2. Select the desired visual report template and click **Edit Template.**
3. In the **Visual Reports - Field Picker** dialog box, add or remove the fields as required.
4. Click **Edit Template.**
5. Save and close the report.

Procedure Reference: Customize a Visual Report by Using the PivotTable Field List Pane

To customize a visual report by using the **PivotTable Field List** pane:

1. Display the desired report in Excel.
2. Click the chart region to display the **PivotTable Field List** pane.
3. Use the **PivotTable Field List** pane to edit the chart further.
   a. On the **Layout** tab, select the layout you want for the **PivotTable Field List** pane.
   b. In the **Choose fields to add to report** list box, select the elements that you wish to add to the chart.
   c. In the **Drag fields between areas below** section, drag the fields from one box to another to filter the report accordingly.
4. Save and close the report.

ACTIVITY 4-2

Customizing a Visual Report

Data Files:

C:\084603Data\Reporting Project Data Visually\CSS Report.mpp

Before You Begin:

The CSS Report.mpp file is open.

Scenario:

Samantha Smith, your colleague, got back to you and asked that you provide her the data for the resources involved in the print phase of the CSS manual project. As you look into the report that you have generated, you decide to add a few more formatting details to make the report a little more attractive and easy to read.

---

1. Display the **Budget Cost Report** in Excel.

    a. On the **Project** tab, click **Visual Reports**.

    b. In the **Visual Reports - Create Report** dialog box, on the **All** tab, select **Budget Cost Report**.

    c. In the **Select level of usage data to include in the report** drop-down list, select **Quarters**.

    d. Click **View** to display the report in Excel.

---

2. Customize the **Budget Cost Report.**

    a. In the adr11 [Compatibility Mode] - Microsoft Excel window, on the Microsoft Office Window Frame, click the **Zoom Out** button to zoom the chart to **80** percent.

    b. The **PivotTable Field List** pane is also displayed. On the **Design** tab, from the **Chart Styles** gallery, select the right-most chart in the fourth row.

    c. In the **PivotTable Field List** pane, in the **Choose fields to add to report** section, scroll down and check the **Resources** check box.

d. Observe that the chart now displays the cost data with respect to each of the resources.

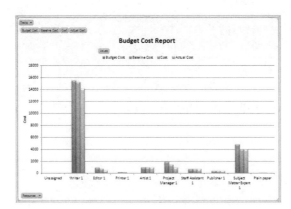

e. In the **Choose fields to add to report** section, check the **Type** check box.

3. Filter resource data in the **PivotTable.**

   a. Click the **Assignment Usage** worksheet to display the **PivotTable.**

   b. In the **PivotTable Field List** pane, in the **Choose fields to add to report** section, click the **Resources** filter drop-down arrow and uncheck the **(Select All)** check box to deselect the options.

   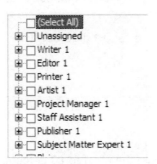

   c. Check the **Writer 1, Editor 1, Printer 1,** and **Project Manager 1** check boxes and click **OK.**

   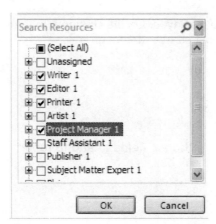

   d. Click the **Chart1** worksheet to display the **Chart** view.

e.   Observe the change in the chart.

f.   Save the Excel workbook as ***My CSS Report1.xlsx*** in the C:\084603Data\Reporting Project Data Visually folder.

g.   Close all windows except Microsoft Project 2010. Do not save the project plan.

TOPIC C
Create a Visual Report Template

In the previous topic, you created and edited visual reports. Over the course of a project, you may have to use similar reports frequently for multiple presentations. Editing them each time could be time consuming, but you can save yourself time by using templates. In this topic, you will create a custom visual report template.

As a project manager, you may have three or more projects in production simultaneously. Although each project is distinct in its own way, you might be expected to follow certain corporate standards in the reports and other documents generated. Manually formatting every report to meet these standards can be time consuming, but having a template that caters to your specific needs addresses this problem.

The Visual Reports — New Template Dialog Box

The **Visual Reports - New Template** dialog box contains options to create a new visual report template.

Figure 4-4: *The Visual Reports — New Template dialog box with options to create a new visual report template.*

Section	Description
Select Application	Allows users to select Excel or Visio as the application where the template is to be created.
Select Data Type	Enables users to specify the data type as one of the six template categories to categorize the custom template accordingly. Choices include **Task Usage, Resource Usage, Assignment Usage, Task Summary, Resource Summary,** and **Assignment Summary.**
Select Fields	Displays the **Visual Report - Field Picker** dialog box. This dialog box enables users to add or remove custom and built-in fields that are to be displayed in the report.

How to Create a Visual Report Template

Procedure Reference: Create an Excel Based Visual Report Template by Using Existing Visual Reports

To create an Excel based visual report template by using existing visual reports:

1. Display the **Visual Reports - Create Report** dialog box.

2. Select the desired report, with specific settings, and click **View.**

3. Customize the Excel workbook to suit your needs.

4. Click the **Microsoft Office** button and choose **Save As.**

5. In the **Save As** dialog box, using the **Save as type** drop-down list, save the report as a template.

   ● Select **Excel 97–2003 Template (*.xlt)** or;

   ● Select **Excel Template (*.xltx).**

6. Enter the desired name for the template.

7. If necessary, navigate to a different location.

8. Click **Save.**

9. In the **Microsoft Office Excel** message box, click **OK** to remove the project-specific information from the workbook.

Procedure Reference: Create an Excel Based Visual Report Template by Editing an Existing Template

To create an Excel based visual report template by editing an existing template:

1. Display the **Visual Reports - Create Report** dialog box.

2. Select the desired report, with specific settings, and click **Edit Template.**

3. In the **Visual Reports - Field Picker** dialog box, add or remove the desired fields and click **Edit Template.**

4. In the Excel workbook, if necessary, customize the report.

5. In the **Save As** dialog box, using the **Save as type** drop-down list, save the report as a template.

   ● Select **Excel 97–2003 Template (*.xlt)** or;

   ● Select **Excel Template (*.xltx).**

Procedure Reference: Create a New Visual Report Template

To create a new visual report template:

1. Display the **Visual Reports - Create Report** dialog box.

2. Click **New Template.**

3. In the **Visual Reports - New Template** dialog box, set the desired settings.

   ● In the **Select Application** section, select **Excel** or **Visio(Metric)** to create a template in that application.

   ● In the **Select Data Type** section, select the type of data you want to use in the report.

   a. Click **Field Picker** to display the **Visual Reports - Field Picker** dialog box.

   b. If necessary, add fields from the **Available Fields** or **Available Custom Fields** list box.

      c.   Remove fields from the **Selected Fields** or **Selected Custom Fields (Maximum of 80)** list box.

      d.   Click **OK.**

4.   Click **OK** to create the report.

5.   If necessary, format the visual report further.

6.   Rename the report and save it.

Custom Visual Report Templates Distribution

If you are ever asked to provide your custom templates to others, all you have to do is provide them the appropriate template (*.xlt or *.xltx) file. Typically, custom templates are stored in the **Documents and Settings***user name***\Application Data\Microsoft\Templates** folder, where *user name* is the user name that is logged on to the computer. This is worth mentioning because the templates that come with Project are stored in a different location on your hard drive, that is, in the **Program Files\Microsoft Office\Templates\1033** folder.

> The first time you save the visual report as a template, it can be saved in any location. To display the custom visual report template along with the predefined visual report templates, you can check the **Include report templates from** check box and select the folder that contains the custom visual report template.

ACTIVITY 4-3
Creating a Visual Report Template

Data Files:

C:\084603Data\Reporting Project Data Visually\CSS Report Template.mpp

Scenario:

Your colleague is pleased with the report you presented to her and asked if you could help others create similar reports for their projects. Instead of working individually on each project's report, you decide to create a template that can be used by everyone to create their reports.

1. Display the **Visual Reports - New Template** dialog box.

    a. From the C:\084603Data\Reporting Project Data Visually folder, open the CSS Report Template.mpp file.

    b. On the **Project** tab, select **Visual Reports.**

    c. In the **Visual Reports - Create Report** dialog box, click **New Template.**

2. Create an **Assignment Usage** report in Excel.

    a. In the **Visual Reports - New Template** dialog box, in the **Select Application** section, verify that **Excel** is selected.

    b. In the **Select Data Type** section, from the **Choose the data on which you want to report** drop-down list, select **Assignment Usage.**

    c. In the **Select Fields** section, click **Field Picker.**

    d. In the **Visual Reports - Field Picker** dialog box, observe the default fields that are selected and click **OK.**

    e. Click **OK** to create the Excel report.

3. Format the **PivotTable** report.

    a. In the **PivotTable Field List** pane, in the **Choose fields to add to report** list box, check the **Actual Cost, Baseline Cost,** and **Cost** check boxes.

    b. Scroll down and check the **Resources** and **Weekly Calendar** check boxes.

c. In the **Drag Fields between areas below** section, from the **Row Labels** list box, drag **Resources** to the **Report Filter** list box.

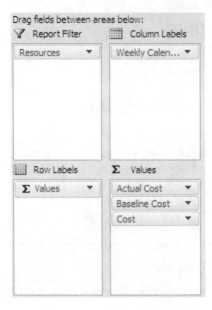

4. Create a **PivotChart**.

a. In the **PivotTable Tools** group on the Ribbon, click the **Options** tab.

b. In the **Tools** group, click **PivotChart.**

c. In the dialog box, observe that **Column chart** is selected and click **OK.** Observe that a PivotChart is created on the same sheet as a PivotTable.

d. Observe that a PivotChart is inserted based on the data in the PivotTable.

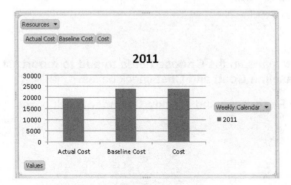

5. Save the report as a template.

a. Click **File** and choose **Save As.**

b. In the **Save As** dialog box, in the **File name** text box, type *My Report Template*

c. In the **Save as type** drop-down list, verify that **Excel Template (*.xltx)** is selected.

d. If necessary, navigate to the C:\Program Files\Microsoft Office\Templates folder.

e. Click **Save.**

f. In the **Microsoft Excel** dialog box, click **Yes.**

g. Close the report template and the **Visual Reports — Create Report** dialog box and then close the project plan without saving.

Lesson 4 Follow-up

In this lesson, you created and edited a visual report. You also created a custom visual report template. Presenting project data visually helps better reader comprehension and ensures retained attention.

1. **When do you think you might represent a project plan as a visual report?**

2. **Of the built-in visual report templates provided in Project, which one do you think you will use most frequently on the job?**

5 | Reusing Project Plan Information

Lesson Time: 1 hour(s), 30 minutes

Lesson Objectives:

In this lesson, you will reuse project plan information.

You will:

- Create a template based on an existing project plan.
- Create a custom view.
- Make custom views available to other project plans using the Organizer.
- Share resources among project plans.
- Create a master project incorporating the existing project plans.

Introduction

Previously, you have worked extensively on your project, updating the plan, creating custom tables and visual reports. Some of the components in the current project may be needed in other projects as well. In this lesson, you will use Project to leverage existing project plan elements for use in other projects.

Many projects share common elements. For instance, formatting of reports may stay consistent across an organization's various projects, or a custom view may gain traction and become popular among project managers. Each project, though unique in its details, may share its basic tasks and resources with other projects. It is far easier to reuse content created in other projects than it is to create project plans from scratch each time.

TOPIC A
Create a Project Plan Template

As you build more and more project plans, you may find yourself repeating certain steps each time. Sharing these objects across projects can help save a great deal of time. In this topic, you will include such common elements in a new project plan template file.

Every organization has a corporate standard that needs to be met in each of its documents. Formatting similar settings for each project plan is a tiring and a repetitive process; also, there are chances that you may miss out on some formats. Having a template that can be used across all your projects helps ensure that things are automatically formatted properly, and that reusable elements are actually reused.

Project Templates

Definition:

A *project template* is a project file that contains generic project information, project plan setup, and formatting information. A template always contains critical information that is common to many projects and lacks additional or nice-to-have information. Project templates may be predefined or custom.

Example:

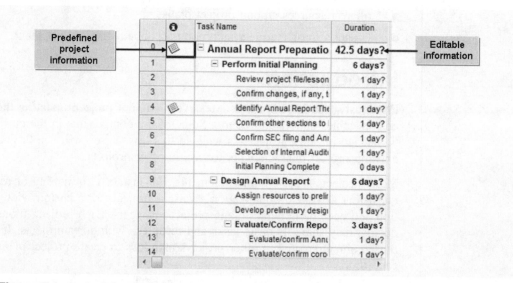

Figure 5-1: A predefined template.

The Global.mpt Template

The global template, Global.mpt, which is sometimes called the global file is the generic Project template that contains default settings on which all new project plans are based. Typically, the Global.mpt file determines the view that will be displayed at startup, the units of work displayed (hours, days, or weeks) in a plan, and whether schedule calculations are performed automatically or manually. The Global.mpt template may also include custom elements deemed necessary by your company.

How to Create a Project Plan Template

Procedure Reference: Create a Project Plan Template from an Existing Project Plan

To create a project plan template from an existing project plan:

1. Open the project plan that you wish to convert into a template.

2. Remove the project-specific data to make it generic.

3. Choose **File→Save As.**

4. Give the template a descriptive name.

5. From the **Save as type** drop-down list, select **Template (*.mpt).**

 As soon as you select the *.mpt option from the drop-down list, the directory automatically changes to the Templates folder within the subdirectory of the user's Application Data folder.

6. Click **Save.**

7. In the current project plan, select data that is to be omitted from the template.

8. Click **Save** again.

9. Close the template.

10. If necessary, open the template again to verify its contents.

Modify a Custom Project Template

If you wish to modify a custom template, you can do so by opening it and adding or deleting the desired elements and saving it as a new custom template, or by overwriting the older one. Any modification you make will not be reflected in any project plan that may have initially used the template. Only new project plans based on the updated template will reflect the changes.

ACTIVITY 5-1
Creating a Template from an Existing Project Plan

Data Files:

C:\084603Data\Reusing Project Plan Information\CSS Week13.mpp

Scenario:

The CSS Training Manual project plan is nearing completion and it already contains the majority of elements you may want to use the next time you and your team members are called upon to create a basic technological training manual. To save yourself time and effort on working on similar projects in the future, you decide to base a new, project-generic template on the latest CSS project plan file.

1. Remove project-specific information from the plan.

   a. From the C:\084603Data\Reusing Project Plan Information folder, open the CSS Week13.mpp file.

   b. Double-click task 0, change the title from **CSS Training Manual** to *Training Manual* and press **Enter.**

   c. Right-click task 18 and choose **Hyperlink→Clear Hyperlinks.**

   d. Double-click task 9, click the **Advanced** tab, set the constraint type to **As Soon As Possible**, clear the constraint date, and click **OK.**

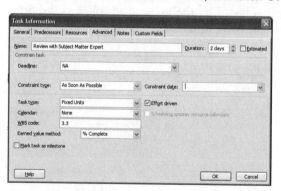

2. Save the project plan as a template.

   a. Click the **File** tab and choose **Save As.**

   b. In the **File name** text box, type *My Training Manual*

   c. From the **Save as type** drop-down list, select **Project Template (*.mpt).**

   d. Click **Save.**

e. In the **Save As Template** dialog box, check the **Values of all baselines, Actual Values,** and **Whether tasks have been published to Project Server** check boxes to omit data from the template.

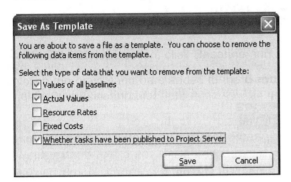

f. Click **Save.**

g. Close the template file.

h. In the **Microsoft Office Project** message box, click **Yes.**

3. View the content of the custom template.

a. Choose **File→New.**

b. In the **Available Templates** section, click the **My templates** link.

c. In the **New** dialog box, verify that **My Training Manual.mpt** is selected and click **OK.**

d. Observe the contents in the project plan.

e. Close the project plan without saving it.

TOPIC B

Create a Custom View

In the previous topic, you saved an existing project plan as a template, which enables you to use that customized structure in other project plans. A customized view is another item that you may want to create and share between plans in Project. In this topic, you will create a custom view that can be saved inside a plan as well as in the global template.

While working on a high-priority project, you may have the need to view various data in different columns simultaneously. Switching views can be a tiresome task, and you may also lose track of what you are doing. To accomplish what you need, you can customize the view so that the information you want to see is displayed. Having that view available in your project plan, or globally on your system, allows for increased efficiency.

The Define New View Dialog Box

The **Define New View** dialog box contains options to specify the type of view you need to create.

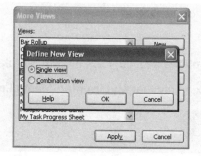

Figure 5-2: The Define New View dialog box with options to create a custom view.

View	Description
Single view	Displays the **View Definition** dialog box. This dialog box contains options that enables users to specify the properties of the specific custom view.
Combination view	Displays the **View Definition** dialog box. This dialog box enables users to select the two tables that are to be displayed in the **Combination view.**

Copy Existing Views

Rather than creating a view from scratch, you can modify a copy of an existing view. You should first create a copy of the existing view in the **More Views** dialog box. Doing so, preserves the original view, while creating the new view definition in the open project plan.

Single View Definition Options

When you select the **Single View Definition** option from the **Define New View** dialog box, you are presented with a set of display choices for your custom view. From here, you can assign a name to your custom view, and control the values for the **Screen, Table, Group,** and **Filter** options.

How to Create a Custom View

Procedure Reference: Create a Custom Single View

To create a custom single view:

1. Select the **View** tab and then choose **Other Views→More Views.**
2. In the **More Views** dialog box, click **New.**
3. In the **Define New View** dialog box, select **Single view** and click **OK.**
4. In the **View Definition** dialog box, specify the settings for the custom view.
   - In the **Name** text box, enter a descriptive name for the new single view.
   - From the **Screen** drop-down list, select a screen type.
   - From the **Table** drop-down list, select the table to be displayed.
   - If necessary, from the **Group** drop-down list, select the desired group for tasks.
   - If necessary, from the **Filter** drop-down list, select the desired filter for the tasks.
5. Check **Highlight Filter** if you want the items that meet the filter criteria to look different from other items when you apply the view.
6. Check **Show in Menu** if you want the custom view to be available from the menu.
7. Click **OK.** The view is saved in the current file and in the global template (global.mpt).

Procedure Reference: Create a Custom Combination View

To create a custom combination view:

1. Select the **View** tab and then choose **Other Views→More Views.**
2. In the **More Views** dialog box, click **New.**
3. In the **Define New View** dialog box, select **Combination view** and click **OK.**
4. In the **View Definition** dialog box, specify the settings for the custom table.
   - In the **Name** text box, enter a descriptive name for the new combination view.
   - In the **Views displayed** section, from the **Primary View** drop-down list, select the view to be displayed in the top pane.
   - From the **Details Pane** drop-down list, select the view to be displayed in the bottom pane.
5. Check **Show in Menu** if you want the custom view to be available from the menu.
6. Click **OK** to create the custom view. The view is saved in the current file and in the global template (global.mpt).

Sorting

Before creating a custom view, check to make sure that you cannot address your need by sorting the existing project plan information differently. On the **View** tab, select **Sort.** You can either sort by **Start Date, Finish Date, Priority, Cost,** or **ID.** If those sorting features do not meet your needs, you can also launch the **Sort** dialog box and choose different methods of sorting project plan data. Even if you end up creating a custom view, you can add lots of additional display options by adjusting the Sort feature of your custom view.

Data Files:

C:\084603Data\Reusing Project Plan Information\New Training Manual.mpp

Scenario:

Earlier, when you updated the task progress for the CSS Training Manual project, you switched views and displayed the **Tracking** table. However, it was not readily apparent how the progress affected the project plan. To see this, you had to switch back to the **Tracking Gantt** view. For the sake of efficiency, you want to enter data directly in the **Tracking** table while viewing the **Tracking Gantt** chart.

1. Create a single view, using the **Tracking** table from the **Task Sheet** view.

   a. From the C:\084603Data\Reusing Project Plan Information folder, open the New Training Manual.mpp file.

   b. On the **View** tab, choose **Other Views→More Views.**

   c. In the **More Views** dialog box, click **New.**

   d. In the **Define New View** dialog box, verify that **Single view** is selected and click **OK.**

   e. In the **View Definition in 'New Training Manual.mpp'** dialog box, in the **Name** text box, type *My Task Progress Sheet*

   f. Verify that the screen is the **Gantt** chart, and from the **Table** drop-down list, select **Tracking.**

   g. From the **Group** drop-down list, select **No Group.**

   h. From the **Filter** drop-down list, select **All Tasks** and click **OK.**

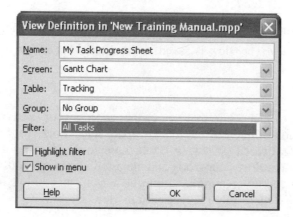

   i. In the **More Views** dialog box, verify that **My Task Progress Sheet** is selected and click **Apply.**

2. **How does the single custom view help you enter task progress data?**

   a) It requires you to switch views frequently to view task information.

   b) It provides a cluttered display of the columns and the charts.

   c) It displays the Tracking table in the Task Sheet view thereby enabling you to view task progress as you enter the progress information.

   d) It creates two separate views to display the progress information.

3. Create a combination view to display both the **Tracking Gantt** view and the **My Task Progress Sheet** view simultaneously.

   a. On the **View** tab, choose **Other Views→More Views.**

   b. In the **More Views** dialog box, click **New.**

   c. In the **Define New View** dialog box, select **Combination view** and click **OK.**

   d. In the **View Definition in 'New Training Manual.mpp'** dialog box, in the **Name** text box, type *My Tracking View*

   e. In the **Views displayed** section, from the **Primary View** drop-down list, select **Tracking Gantt.**

   f. From the **Details Pane** drop-down list, select **My Task Progress Sheet** and click **OK.**

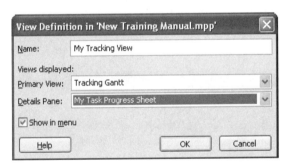

4. View the project plan in the combination view.

   a. In the **More Views** dialog box, verify that **My Tracking View** is selected.

   b. Click **Apply** to display the new combination view.

   c. Observe the content in the combination view. Save the plan as *My New Training Manual.mpp* and close it.

TOPIC C
Make Custom Views Available to Other Project Plans

In the previous topic, you created a custom combination view for your project, and saved it in your plan and in the global template. Once it is created and saved, you can use it in other project files. In this topic, you will make custom views available to other project plans.

Being able to use custom views or other custom elements in other plans will make some work a lot simpler. You could add the view to a template, but in many cases, custom views are a matter of preference rather than a requirement. Using the same view in another plan ensures that the custom views will be identical, so that information will be displayed exactly as it was in the original plan.

The Organizer

The *Organizer* is a tool for copying, deleting, and renaming project elements such as calendars, reports, tables, and views. To copy elements between any two project plans or template files, both the source file and the destination file must be opened with the file name displayed in the **Available In** drop-down list. The **Organizer** can be launched by clicking the **File** tab, then the **Info** tab, and then the **Organizer** button. It can also be launched from other locations where you would be likely to customize elements, such as the **Custom Reports, More Views,** and **More Tables** dialog boxes.

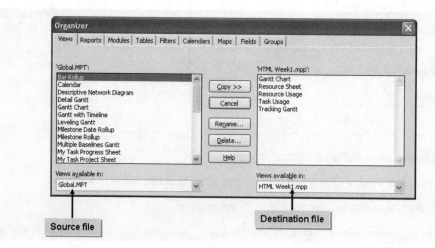

Figure 5-3: *The Organizer with options displayed.*

How to Make Custom Views Available to Other Project Plans

Procedure Reference: Make Custom Views Available to Other Project Plans

To make custom views available to other project plans:

1. If the view is stored in a project plan file and not in the global template, open the project plan that currently contains the custom view or views—the source file project plan.

2. Open the project plan that will receive the custom view or views—the destination file project plan.

3. Display the **Organizer.**

   - Select the **View** tab and then choose **Other Views→More Views,** and in the **More Views** dialog box, click **Organizer** or;

   - Select the **File** tab and then choose **Info→Organizer** or;

   - Select the **View** tab and then choose **Tables→More Tables,** and in the **More Tables** dialog box, click **Organizer.**

4. If necessary, select the **Views** tab.

5. On the left side of the **Organizer,** from the **Views available in** drop-down list, select the source file project plan.

6. On the right side of the **Organizer,** from the **Views available in** drop-down list, select the destination project plan file.

7. In the list box on the left, select the custom view or views.

8. Click **Copy.**

9. Click **Close.**

Copying Other Elements

The **Organizer** can be used to share resources other than views between project plans. The only change is to select the appropriate element's tab in the **Organizer** dialog box and then select that element. For instance, if you want to copy a custom table from one plan to another, you would display the **Organizer** dialog box, select the **Tables** tab, select the custom table from the source file project plan's list and then click **Copy.**

ACTIVITY 5-3
Copying Custom Views

Data Files:

C:\084603Data\Reusing Project Plan Information\HTML Training Manual.mpp

Scenario:

Your next project, the HTML Training Manual, is getting ready to start. Before you begin, you want to share the project plan with a coworker who does not have the same global.mpt file as you, and therefore cannot take advantage of the two custom views that you just created: **My Task Progress Sheet** and **My Tracking View.**

---

1. Copy **My Task Progress Sheet** and **My Tracking View** into the HTML Training Manual file.

   a. From the C:\084603Data\Reusing Project Plan Information folder, open the HTML Training Manual.mpp file.

   b. In the HTML Training Manual.mpp file, select the **View** tab and then choose **Other Views→More Views.**

   c. Click **Organizer** to display the **Organizer** dialog box.

   d. Verify that the **Views** tab is selected, and on the left side of the **Organizer** dialog box, from the **Views available in** drop-down list, verify that **Global.MPT** is selected.

   e. If necessary, on the right side of the **Organizer** dialog box, from the **Views available in** drop-down list, select **HTML Training Manual.mpp.**

   f. In the **Global.MPT** list box, select **My Task Progress Sheet** and **My Tracking View.**

   g. Click **Copy** to copy the two custom views to the other project plan.

---

2. View the custom views in the HTML Training Manual.mpp file.

   a. Click **Close** to close the **Organizer.**

   b. In the **More Views** dialog box, select **My Tracking View** and click **Apply** to apply the view.

   c. Close the **More Views** dialog box.

   d. Save the plan as *My HTML Training Manual.mpp* and close any open project plans.

TOPIC D
Share Resources

In the previous topic, you shared custom views created in one project with another. Another thing you may need to share with other project plans is information about the resources that may be working on multiple projects. In this topic, you will share resources.

Rarely are a plan's resources fully your own. It is quite common for your team members to be part of a larger pool of resources because they may be working on project plans other than yours. Sharing resources allows you to schedule work across projects while enabling you to track and manage resource conflicts. This prevents the resource from becoming over allocated. If you don't share resources properly, you could unknowingly end up scheduling a person for double duty, not only burning the person out, but perhaps creating tension between yourself and other project managers who use the same resources.

Resource Pools

A *resource pool* is a separate Project file that contains only resource information such as names, rates, and so on that you can assign to tasks in one or more project plans. Each project plan that uses the resources listed in the resource pool is called a *sharer file*. Resource pools provide sharer files with a centralized, consistent, and current source of resource information, thereby helping to prevent resource over allocation. Resource pools also eliminate the need for the project managers to re-enter resource information.

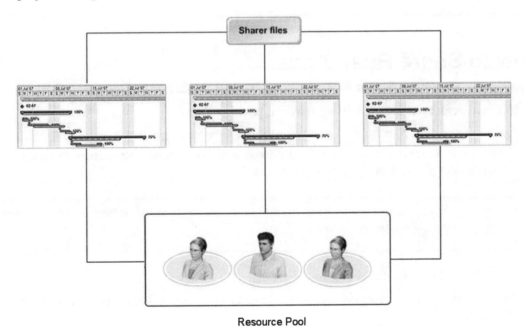

Figure 5-4: The different sharer files sharing resources from the same pool.

 When saving a new resource pool, it is a good idea to put the words "Resource Pool" or "RP" somewhere in the file name so that it can be distinguished from other project plans.

Sharer Projects

A *sharer project* is an actual project that may contain resources that you want to use in another project plan or sharer file. Unlike a resource pool, which contains only resource information, a sharer project contains tasks, costs, duration information, and so on. In effect, the sharer project becomes a resource pool; however, in a sharer project, the ability to monitor resource allocation is limited to just the linked plans.

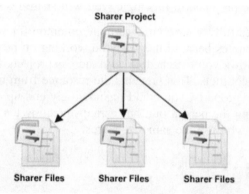

Sharer Project

Sharer Files   **Sharer Files**   **Sharer Files**

Figure 5-5: The sharer projects's resources shared between different sharer files.

 Microsoft documentation sometimes uses the terms "sharer project" and "sharer file" interchangeably. This course will use "sharer project" to mean a plan that is a source of resources, and "sharer file" to mean a plan that utilizes those resources.

How to Share Resources

Procedure Reference: Share Resources by Using an Existing Resource Pool

To share resources by using an existing resource pool:

1. Open the resource pool file that you want to use, as a read-only file.

2. Select the **Resources** tab and then choose **Resource Pool→Share Resources** to verify which project plans, if any, are sharing the pool.

 If the resource pool is already linked to a sharer file, you will be prompted to open the resource pool as read only.

3. Open the project plan that will share the resources—the sharer file.

4. In the sharer project, select the **Resources** tab and then choose **Resource Pool→Share Resources.**

 You can also display the **Resource Management** toolbar and click the **Share Resources** button.

5. Select **Use Resources (requires at least one open resource pool).**

6. From the **From** drop-down list, select the desired open resource pool file.

7. If necessary, give the resource pool precedence.

8. Click **OK.**

9. Assign resources to tasks in the sharer file.

10. If necessary, level the resources.

11. Save and close the sharer file.

12. Save and close the resource pool.

The Open Resource Pool Options

When you open a resource pool that is shared by other project plans, you have a few options. You can open the resource pool as read only. Most often, you will use this option because it allows others to work on project plans linked to the pool. If you need to modify the resource pool, you should open it in the read-write mode; this lets you directly save edits to the pool, but it prevents sharer files from updating the resource pool.

Precedence

By default, if conflicts arise between a sharer file and a resource pool, the resource pool will overwrite the resource information in the sharer file because the resource pool has precedence over the sharer file. For instance, if a sharer file states that Editor 1 makes $20/hour and the resource pool states that Editor 1 makes $25/hour, the $20 rate in the sharer file will be over-written by the resource pool's data–$25/hour rate. Ordinarily, it is preferable to give precedence to the resource pool; however, if a project plan is considered critical, the sharer file may be given precedence.

Discontinue Sharing Resources

If the time comes when you want to stop sharing resources with a resource pool or sharer project, you can do so by selecting the **Use Own Resources** option in the **Share Resources** dialog box. When you disconnect from a resource pool, the sharer file retains assignment and resource information.

ACTIVITY 5-4

Sharing Resources by Using a Resource Pool

Data Files:

C:\084603Data\Reusing Project Plan Information\TM Resource Pool.mpp, C:\084603Data\ Reusing Project Plan Information\XML Training Manual.mpp

Scenario:

Your organization is essentially divided into four teams. All projects freely and regularly utilize the members of these teams as their resources. Currently, you have a project that needs to have resources assigned to tasks; however, because you do not have a team of your own, you need to make sure you do not overallocate shared resources between projects.

---

1. Display the **Share Resources** dialog box.

    a. From the C:\084603Data\Reusing Project Plan Information folder, open the TM Resource Pool.mpp file as a read-only file.

    b. On the **Resource** tab, choose **Resource Pool→Share Resources.**

    c. Observe the project plans that are currently sharing the resource pool.

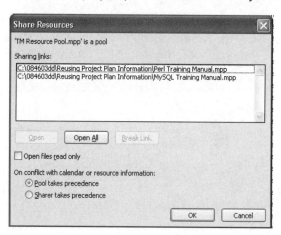

    d. Click **Cancel** to close the **Share Resources** dialog box.

---

2. Share the resources in the TM Resource Pool file with the XML Training Manual file.

    a. Open the XML Training Manual project plan.

    b. Display the **Share Resources** dialog box.

    c. Select **Use resources (requires at least one open resource pool).**

d. Verify that **TM Resource Pool.mpp** appears in the **From** drop down list, and that **Pool takes precedence** is selected.

e. Click **OK** to make the resource in the resource pool available within the XML Training Manual project plan.

3. Assign and level the resources for the XML Training Manual project plan.

   a. If necessary, switch to the **Gantt Chart** view.

   b. Adjust the **Gantt** chart and the columns to display the **Resource Names** column.

   c. In the **Resource Names** column, for task 2, assign Project Manager 2.

   d. For task 4, assign Project Manager 2 and Subject Matter Expert 2, and for task 5, assign Writer 1.

   e. Click in the cell below the current cell.

   f. Select the **Resource** tab and click **Level All.** Observe that the dates for the project have been pushed out because Writer 1 is now overallocated.

   g. If necessary, in the **Microsoft Office Project** message box, click **Skip.**

4. Reassign task 5 to Writer 2.

   a. In the **Resource Names** column, assign task 5 to Writer 2.

   b. Click in the cell below the current cell.

   c. Level the resources again. Observe that the dates for the project plan are moved back in because Writer 2 is not overallocated.

   d. If necessary, in the **Microsoft Office Project** message box, click **Skip.**

   e. Save the project plan as *My XML Training Manual.mpp*

   f. Click **OK** to update the resource pool to reflect changes for all open sharer files.

   g. Close the My XML Training Manual.mpp file.

   h. In the **Microsoft Office Project** dialog box, if necessary, click **Yes** and then click **OK.**

5. View the sharer files.

   a. In the TM Resource Pool project plan, display the **Share Resources** dialog box.

b.   Observe that the resources are now shared with the XML Training Manual.mpp file.

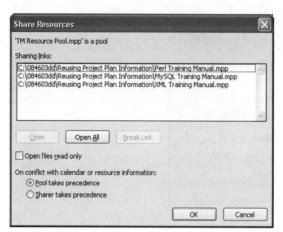

c.   Click **Cancel** to close the **Share Resources** dialog box.

d.   Close the resource pool.

TOPIC E
Create a Master Project

In the previous topic, you shared resources with other project plans. As a project manager, you may have to work with multiple projects simultaneously. Managing one project plan can be challenging by itself, but monitoring multiple project plans can be even more intimidating. In this topic, you will combine several plans into one master project.

Putting related projects under one roof gives you the ability to work conveniently with these projects as if they were one large, consolidated project plan. You could allocate resources, apply filters, and analyze costs separately for each project and then try to reconcile any problem in each file. It is much more convenient, however, to combine them in a master plan and do these procedures once. You will likely make fewer errors and you will instantly see how one change will impact the related plans.

Master Projects

Definition:

A *master project* is a project file that contains other inserted projects. Each inserted project is called a *subproject*. Master projects embed subprojects into them. Master projects may or may not have content of their own. The subprojects in the master project file are linked to the original project file. Master projects are typically used as a way to consolidate smaller, related projects or phases into one plan so that they can be viewed, updated, and monitored more easily.

Example:

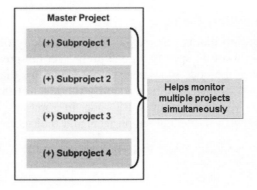

Figure 5-6: Subprojects within a master project.

Master Projects and the Critical Path

By default, Microsoft Project treats subprojects as summary tasks, so a single critical path is created that covers all projects in the master project plan. To turn this feature off, select the **File** tab, then select **Options,** and then select **Schedule.** Scroll down to **Calculation options for this project** and uncheck the box that reads **Inserted projects are calculated like summary tasks.**

Break the Link Between the Master and Subproject

Sometimes, you may not want the changes you make to the master project to be reflected in your local copies of the subprojects. You can break the link between the subproject and its source file by selecting the subproject's summary task and displaying its **Task Information** dialog box. On the **Advanced** tab, deselect the **Link To Project** option to unlink the two.

WBS Codes

The Work Breakdown Structure codes or *WBS codes* are alphanumeric codes that help users identify specific tasks in the outline of a project. Project supports two types of WBS codes: Outline numbers and Custom. For a custom code, you can define your own code mask, which establishes the sequence of numbers, letters, or other characters that you want to use for each level in your WBS hierarchy.

 When using a master document, you should insert the WBS codes into the subprojects before they are inserted into the master project.

 The **RBS**, or Resource Breakdown Structure, is similar to a **WBS**. However, the RBS is used to organize the structure outline for resources.

 Project does not provide built-in WBS charts. However, an add-on product can be used to create a WBS chart from a Microsoft Office Project file.

The WBS Code Definition Dialog Box

The **WBS Code Definition** dialog box enables users to specify the WBS code masks and their formats. The user can choose to specify a code prefix, set the prescribed number of characters for each level, or change the code separator symbol using this dialog box. Different code separators for different levels of tasks can help identify the level of the task. A code prefix enables users to identify the highest level of the WBS code. In a master project, these code prefixes can be used to identify each individual subprojects and their corresponding tasks.

There are four categories of characters that you can use in the different levels of your custom code mask.

Code Mask	Description
Numbers (Ordered)	Uses a numerical code to represent the breakdown structure.
Uppercase Letter (Ordered)	Uses uppercase letters as codes to represent the breakdown structure.
Lowercase Letters (Ordered)	Uses lowercase letters as codes to represent the breakdown structure.
Characters (Unordered)	Uses a combination of numbers, letters, and special characters as codes to represent the breakdown structure. By default, the asterisk is used as the first symbol.

How to Create a Master Project

Procedure Reference: Create a Master Plan

To create a master plan:

1. Open the file that will become the master project.
2. In the **Gantt Chart** view, select the row below the task where you want to insert the sub-project.
3. Choose **Project→Subproject.**
4. Locate the desired project plan file.
5. Click **Insert** to insert the project plan as a subproject.
6. Indent the subproject, so that the master project becomes a summary task including the newly inserted subproject.
7. Display the subproject to ensure that all the tasks are inserted.
8. Repeat the above steps, as needed.

Procedure Reference: Create a Custom WBS Code

To create a custom WBS code:

1. Insert the **WBS** column.
2. Select the **Project** tab and then choose **WBS→Define Code.**
3. In the **WBS Code Definition** dialog box, specify the desired format for the code mask.
   - In the **Project Code Prefix** text box, enter the desired code prefix that will be seen along with the WBS code mask.
   - In the **Code mask (excluding prefix)** section, in the **Sequence** column, from the drop-down list, select the desired type of character.
   - In the **Length** column, specify the number of alphanumeric characters for that level of the mask.
   - In the **Separator** column, specify the desired WBS code separator to insert between levels of the mask. The default separator is a period.
4. Click **OK** to use the specified code mask as the format for the WBS codes.

The Project Field

One of the difficulties in working within a master project is being able to identify the tasks that belong to each subproject. There is, however, an easy way to fix this in the **Entry** table of the **Gantt Chart** view. Insert the **Project** field as a column next to the **Task Name** column, and the subproject's name will be placed right next to the task itself for easy identification.

ACTIVITY 5-5
Creating a Quarterly Training Manual Master Project

Data Files:

C:\084603Data\Reusing Project Plan Information\Q3 Master.mpp, C:\084603Data\Reusing Project Plan Information\Subproject CSS.mpp, C:\084603Data\Reusing Project Plan Information\Subproject HTML.mpp, C:\084603Data\Reusing Project Plan Information\ Subproject Unix.mpp

Scenario:

It is August 29, 2011, and the third quarter of Our Global Company's fiscal year is in full swing. You are busier than ever, and you have one project plan already in progress, and two new ones will be starting very shortly. You need to find an efficient way to monitor all these plans so nothing slips through the cracks. In the last subproject, the resource assigned to the first task is also working on the last task of the previous subproject. Therefore, he has to complete the previous task before he is available to work on the other project. Additionally, you need to make sure that referring to these tasks in the master project is easy.

1. Create a custom WBS code for the master project.

   a. From the C:\084603Data\Reusing Project Plan Information folder, open the Q3 Master.mpp file.

   b. Insert the **WBS** column to the left of the **Duration** column.

   c. On the **Project** tab, choose **WBS→Define Code.**

   d. In the **WBS Code Definition in 'Q3 Master.mpp'** dialog box, in the **Code mask (excluding prefix)** section, in the **Sequence** column, from the first drop-down list, select **Uppercase Letters (ordered).**

   e. In the **Project Code Prefix** text box, type *master project -* and press the **Spacebar.**

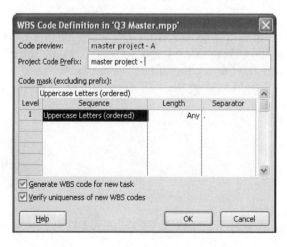

   f. Click **OK.**

g. If necessary, adjust the **WBS** column to display the code.

2. Insert the CSS subproject into the Q3 Master project.

a. In the **Gantt Chart** view, below the project summary task, in the second row, select the **Task Name** field.

b. Click **Subproject.**

c. If necessary, navigate to the C:\084603Data\Reusing Project Plan Information folder and select **Subproject CSS.mpp.**

d. Click **Insert.**

e. If necessary, click the minus sign **(-)** to hide the tasks.

f. In the **1 Subproject CSS** row, observe that the WBS code automatically updates to **master project - A.**

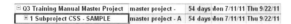

3. Add the Subproject HTML.mpp and Subproject Unix.mpp files as subprojects to the master project.

a. In the third row, select the **Task Name** field.

b. Click **Subproject.**

c. Select **Subproject HTML.mpp** and click **Insert.**

d. Similarly, insert Subproject Unix.mpp as a subproject.

e. Observe that all the projects are added as subprojects.

4. Link tasks within two subprojects.

a. Display all the tasks in all the subprojects.

b. Select the tasks **Subproject 2– 1.8** and **Subproject 3– 1.1.**

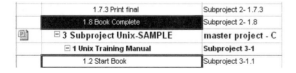

    c.   On the **Task** tab, in the **Schedule** group, click **Link Tasks.**

5.   View the **Project Summary** report.

    a.   On the **Project** tab, click **Reports.**

    b.   Verify that **Overview** is selected and click **Select.**

    c.   Verify that **Project Summary** is selected and click **Select.**

    d.   Zoom in on the report.

    e.   Close the print preview window and the other dialog boxes.

    f.   Save the master project as *My Q3 Master.mpp* and close all the project plans.

    g.   Click **Yes to all** to save the changes to the subprojects.

Lesson 5 Follow-up

In this lesson, you shared specific project information across various other project plans. Reusing project information helps you save time and effort.

1. **What are the benefits of reusing project plan elements? What elements might you reuse?**

2. **Is your company likely to use resource pools to help monitor resource usage? Give reasons.**

Follow-up

In this course, you have successfully exchanged project plan data with other applications, updated project plans, created visual reports, and reused project plan information. With these skills, you can now communicate more effectively with stakeholders and team members as you monitor, correct, and report on a project plan throughout its life cycle.

What's Next?

Microsoft® Project 2010: Level 2 is the last course in this series. If you wish to increase your project management skills, you might consider additional training in professional project management, such as *Project Management Professional (PMP®) Certification: Fourth Edition* or *CompTIA® Project+™ Certification (2009 Objectives)*.

A | Synchronizing with SharePoint

TOPIC A

Sync Project Information with SharePoint

SharePoint provides project managers with a wide range of tools that enable sharing of data in both applications. As a project manager, you must recognize the potential of using external information sources to build and manage your project plan. Your team members can view and modify the project information in SharePoint site and then you can synchronize the updates by clicking the **Sync** button in Project Professional 2010. If the same data is modified both in SharePoint site and Project Professional 2010, you will be prompted with a conflict resolution dialog during the Sync operation.

SharePoint Synchronization

 If resources are associated with tasks, the resources must be set up in SharePoint as users with the same name in order for them to be accepted into the SharePoint task list.

Synchronizing Project with SharePoint happens in both directions. If you make changes in the project plan, you can synchronize those changes back to the SharePoint Project tasks list. Additionally, when you sync, automatically scheduled tasks are converted to manually scheduled because in SharePoint, all tasks are manually scheduled.

Default Fields Set to Sync

By default, only the following fields are set to sync.

- Name
- Start
- Finish
- % Complete
- Resource Names
- Predecessor

How to Sync Project Information with SharePoint

Procedure Reference: Synchronize a Project Plan with a SharePoint Project Task List

To synchronize a Project plan with a SharePoint list:

 The syncing features work only with SharePoint Foundation 2010 and SharePoint Server 2010 and the features are available only in Project Professional 2010.

1. Open the Project plan that you wish to publish to a SharePoint list.
2. Click **File** and then click **Save & Send.**
3. Click **Sync with Tasks Lists.**
4. In the **Site URL** list, choose the URL of the SharePoint site that you want to sync with.
5. Click **Validate URL.** If prompted, provide the credentials required to connect to the SharePoint site.
6. In the **Select an existing tasks list** list, choose the name of the SharePoint task list you want the project tasks list to sync with. You can add a new list by typing the name.
7. Click **Sync.**

Procedure Reference: Import a SharePoint List into Project

To import a SharePoint list into Project:

1. Open the Project plan that you wish to publish to a SharePoint list.
2. Click **File** and then click **Save & Send.**
3. Click **Sync with Tasks Lists.**
4. In the **Site URL** list, choose the URL of the SharePoint site that contains the list you want to use.
5. Click **Validate URL.**
6. In the **Select an existing tasks list** list, choose the name of the SharePoint task list you want to export to Project.
7. Click **Sync.**

Procedure Reference: Add Built-In or Custom Fields to Sync

To add more fields, including built-in or custom fields:

1. Choose the Backstage view of a Project plan you wish to sync.
2. Choose **Info.**
3. In the **Sync to Task Lists** group, choose **Manage Fields→Add Field.**
4. In the **Add Field** dialog box, click the fields you wish to add.
5. When finished, click the **Add Field** button and click **OK.**

Lesson Labs

Lesson labs are provided as an additional learning resource for this course. The labs may or may not be performed as part of the classroom activities. Your instructor will consider setup issues, classroom timing issues, and instructional needs to determine which labs are appropriate for you to perform, and at what point during the class. If you do not perform the labs in class, your instructor can tell you if you can perform them independently as self-study, and if there are any special setup requirements.

Lesson 1 Lab 1

Exchanging Project Plan Information

Activity Time: 5 minutes

Data Files:

Periodicals Phase 1 Draft.mpp, Project Info.xlsx

Scenario:

One of your team members has provided you with information regarding the resources working on one of your projects. You need to add this information to your project plan, and then you need to send a report to your team and your manager. For clarity and convenience, your manager has asked you to provide the information as an image.

1. Open the Phase 1 Draft.mpp file and append the resource information from the Project Info.xlsx file to the project plan.

2. Export the project information as an Excel workbook.

3. Copy a picture of the project information in the **Gantt Chart** view into a Word document.

4. Save the Word document and the project plan and close them.

Lesson 2 Lab 1

Updating a Project Plan

Activity Time: 15 minutes

Data Files:

Update Phase1.mpp

Scenario:

It is Monday, 8/15/11, and phase 1 of the Our Global Company Periodicals plan, Update Phase 1.mpp, has been underway for a week now. You need to update the project plan with the task progress information listed below.

1. Task 3 has been completed and it lasted only one day instead of two.

2. Task 4 was completed a day late because the Business Advisor had a family emergency on Wednesday the 8th and was unavailable for work that day.

3. Task 5 was completed on Friday, but the manager had to put in two hours of overtime work.

To prepare for the upcoming weekly status meeting, you need to create a table based on the **Baseline** table, which contains only baseline and interim dates for tasks.

---

1. From the C:\084603Data\Updating a Project Plan folder, open the Update Phase1.mpp file.

---

2. In the **Gantt Chart** view, in the **Tracking** table, enter task progress information for task 3 to mark it 100% complete with an actual duration of only one day.

---

3. Mark task 4 as 100% complete and split it on Wednesday with an interruption of one day to account for the Business advisor's family emergency.

---

4. In the **Task Usage** view, in the **Work** table, enter task progress information for task 5 to mark it as completed on Friday with two hours of overtime work.

---

5. Set an interim plan for the project.

---

6. Create a custom table named *BASELINE/INTERIM DATES* based on the **Baseline** table with content as specified and display it in the **Gantt Chart** view.

---

7. Display only the completed tasks in the **BASELINE/INTERIM DATES** table.

Lesson 3 Lab 1

Managing Project Costs

Activity Time: 10 minutes

Data Files:

XML Week3.mpp, BudgetTypes.docx

Scenario:

The XML Training Manual project is proceeding as planned. However, some of the costs have changed. Editor 1 has received a salary raise of 15% that takes effect on 10/17/11. Task 23—Print Final will use a more expensive grade of paper that costs $10.00 per ream. You need to update the project plan to reflect these changes. You are also informed that the project plan will be reviewed during the upcoming project status meeting. Your reporting manager asks you to display costs incurred against allowances set through budget resources in the project plan. She also requests you to incorporate a Word document detailing approved company budget types in the project plan.

1.   From the C:\084603Data\Managing Project Costs folder, open the XML Week3.mpp file.

2.   In the **Resource Sheet** view, update the cost rate table **A** for Editor 1 to reflect a base and overtime salary raise of 15% that takes effect on 10/17/11.

3.   Update the cost rate tables for the resource Paper to provide an alternate rate of $10.00 per ream in cost rate table **B.**

4.   In the **Task Usage** view, assign cost rate table **B** to task 23 for the resource Paper.

5.   In the **Resource Usage** view, group costs by budget type.

6.   In the **Gantt Chart** view, link the BudgetTypes.docx file to the project summary task.

Lesson 4 Lab 1

Creating a Custom Visual Report Template

Activity Time: 10 minutes

Data Files:

Reports.mpp

Scenario:

Your manager has asked you to give several upper management stakeholders a briefing about some of your current projects and their progress. She also mentioned that it will be more appealing to present the information using charts and diagrams rather than as raw numbers. Because your organization has decided to hold similar meetings at regular intervals, you might want to reuse the basic content in the reports.

---

1. From the C:\084603Data\Reporting Project Data Visually folder, open the Reports.mpp file.

---

2. Create a report named **Budget Work Report.**

---

3. Format the report to contain data against the resource type information.

---

4. Save the report as **My Reports.xltx.**

Lesson 5 Lab 1

Creating a Master Project with Shared Elements

Activity Time: 10 minutes

Data Files:

New Business Master.mpp, Periodicals Master.mpp, Periodicals Phase 1.mpp, Periodicals Phase 2.mpp, Periodicals Phase 3.mpp, Periodicals Phase 4.mpp

Scenario:

With phase 1 of the Our Global Company's new business plan coming to an end, and with three phases remaining, you need a fast and an efficient way to monitor and report on tasks in all the four phases of the overall project plan.

1. From the C:\084603Data\Reusing Project Plan Information folder, open the New Business Master.mpp file.

2. In the New Business Master project plan, create a new combination view named *GANTT/NETWORK* that shows the **Gantt Chart** on top and the **Network Diagram** below.

3. From the New Business Master project plan, copy the **GANTT/NETWORK** view to the **Periodicals Master.**

4. Insert a **WBS** column in the **Periodicals Master.**

5. Add the four periodical phases as subprojects to the Periodicals Master project.

     There are no links between subprojects in this master project plan. However, because these phases are sequential, you may want to link the last task in each subproject phase to the first actual task in the succeeding phase.

6. Save the master project as *My Periodicals Master.mpp* and save changes to all the subprojects. Close any remaining open project plans.

Solutions

Lesson 2

Activity 2-3

3. When task 7 is split, why is an interruption of three days inserted instead of the default one day?

   a) Due to a constraint on task 7

   b) Due to the task relationship of task 7 and task 8

   ✓ c) Due to the fact that task 7 was split on a Friday

   d) Due to resource limitations for task 7

Lesson 5

Activity 5-2

2. How does the single custom view help you enter task progress data?

   a) It requires you to switch views frequently to view task information.

   b) It provides a cluttered display of the columns and the charts.

   ✓ c) It displays the Tracking table in the Task Sheet view thereby enabling you to view task progress as you enter the progress information.

   d) It creates two separate views to display the progress information.

Glossary

custom field

A way to add additional attributes and functionality to tasks, resources, assignments, or projects.

exporting

A method of transferring data from the application in use to a different application.

filter

A tool that controls the display of information based on specified selection criteria.

groups

A method of organizing the information presented in a view according to specific criteria.

hyperlink

An interactive icon, which, when clicked, links to a location in the current project plan, a file in its corresponding application, a web page in a browser, or a new Message form in Outlook for an email address.

importing

A method of fetching data from a different application to the application in use.

inactive task

A task that is cut from the project timeline, yet does not disappear from the project as a whole.

interim plan

A plan with a copy of the current start and finish dates that can be set once a project is underway.

map

A set of instructions that traces the type of data that is imported or exported into a project plan.

master project

A project file that contains other inserted projects.

Organizer

A tool for copying, deleting, and renaming project elements such as calendars, reports, tables, and views.

overtime work

The extra hours of work put in by employees outside of regular working hours

placeholder tasks

The manually created tasks that a user can create even if they do not have much information associated with them.

progress bars

The thick black lines that get displayed inside the taskbars in the Gantt Chart view showing how much of a task has been completed.

progress line

A line drawn in the chart portion of a view on either the status date or current date.

project template
A project file that contains generic project information, project plan setup, and formatting.

resource pool
A separate Project file that contains only resource information such as names, rates, and so on that can be assigned to tasks in one or more project plans.

sharer file
A project plan that uses the resources listed in the resource pool.

sharer project
An actual project plan that happens to contain some resources you want to use in another project plan or sharer file. In effect, the sharer project becomes a resource pool.

status date
A date other than the current date that is used to check a project's status at a particular point in time.

subproject
A project inserted into a master project.

visual reports
The graphical representation of project data in the form of charts.

WBS codes
(Work Breakdown Structure codes) The alphanumeric codes that help users identify specific tasks in the outline of the project.

Index